LANDMARK COLLECTOR'S LIBRARY

Historic Parks & Gardens of Cheshire

Linden Groves

With photographs by Richard Groves

Welcome to the Cheshire Gardens Trust

CHESHIRE GARDENS ·TRUST·

In April 2004 a group of volunteers created the Cheshire Gardens Trust, which is affiliated to the Association of Gardens Trusts.

The main aim of the Trust is to promote the parks & gardens in Cheshire.

The group will endeavour to improve awareness and appreciation of local garden heritage and promote their conservation and development. It will also attempt to research and record historic designed landscapes. Importantly, the group will encourage the creation of new parks and gardens.

By joining the Cheshire Gardens Trust you will be able to meet people with similar interests; go on guided visits to parks and gardens throughout the UK and attend talks by specialists in all aspects of gardening.

Cheshire Gardens Trust members will receive a regular newsletter with a list of events and various articles of interest.

FOR MORE INFORMATION

and details on how to join, visit our website or write to us using the details below.

www.cheshiregardenstrust.org.uk

The CGT Membership Secretary
11 Carriage Drive, Frodsham, Cheshire WA6 6DU.

Previous page: Herb garden at Eaton Hall, Cheshire. Opposite page: Sandstone gateway in the Temple Garden, at Cholmondeley Castle, Cheshire.

Historic Parks &
Gardens of Cheshire

Linden Groves

Landmark Publishing

Published by

LANDMARK
Publishing Ltd ● ○ ○ ○

Ashbourne Hall, Cokayne Ave
Ashbourne, Derbyshire DE6 1EJ England
Tel: (01335) 347349 Fax: (01335) 347303
e-mail: landmark@clara.net
web site: www.landmarkpublishing.co.uk

1st edition

ISBN 1 84306 124 4

© **Linden Groves 2004**

British Library Cataloguing in Publication Data: a catalogue
record for this book is available from the British Library.

Printed by Gutenberg Press Ltd, Malta

Design & reproduction by Simon Hartshorne

Edited by Kay Coulson

Cover captions:

Front cover: Cholmondeley Castle.
Back cover Top: Mellor's Gardens

Contents

Introduction   6

Map   9

Gawsworth Old Hall   10

Cholmondeley Castle   18

Dunham Massey   30

Adlington Hall   42

Lyme Park   50

Tatton Park   58

Eaton Hall   70

Arley Hall   82

Crewe Hall   91

Dorfold Hall   98

Rode Hall   106

Birkenhead Park   114

Grosvenor Park   122

Queen's Park   126

Mellor's Gardens   134

Peover Hall   142

Ness Botanic Gardens   150

Thornton Manor & Port Sunlight   157

Tirley Garth   166

Index   173

Introduction

Cheshire is certainly one of those counties for whom the words a 'green and pleasant land' could have been written. Indeed, surveying the scene from one of its few high points say, Mow Cop or Lyme Park, it is difficult not to hear them even in the wind. As with any county, the topography is varied, but the enduring image of Cheshire is of rich green fields, gentle slopes, and narrow lanes, endowed with a generous quantity of traditional black and white houses and smart halls, many enjoying beautiful gardens. With a friendly climate and fertile soil, this is a county that can enjoy its gardening, although in all corners there seems to be a disappointment in the performance of roses!

It is clear, both from looking through dusty archives and through visiting gardens, that my affection for Cheshire is shared by many, as few who live there, be it in the eighteenth or the twenty-first centuries, have had an urge to stray over its boundaries. I have been touched to discover whilst writing this book that many of the gardeners seem to stay at the same property for most of their working careers and if they do change, they often simply move to another garden in Cheshire. Hence, the Head Gardener at Ness used to work at Arley, one of the gardeners at Adlington is the son of the Head Gardener at Tatton, and, encouragingly, the son of the Head Gardener at Peover works with his father whilst studying horticulture.

Deciding recently to promote its horticultural assets, the county council has begun to proclaim that Cheshire gardens attract one in eight garden visits made in Great Britain. My hope is that this book will demonstrate why this should be no surprise. Cheshire has been a county of garden lovers for many centuries, and their endeavours have left us with many treasures. Some of these are still in stunning condition, albeit with a different face to that of the past, some are showing their age, and some are currently 'sleeping', perhaps to be revived at a later date but at the moment offering only a tantalising reminder of what they once were. Others have sadly been lost forever to decay, development, or perhaps simply many centuries' worth of redesign. These I have left out of this book, not without some regret, choosing instead to focus on those parks and gardens of which some element still remains as it once was, even if it is only an outline under rough grass. Inevitably for a book that can contain only a handful of sites, there will be some that readers will be surprised to find missing, whichever I chose to include. For this I can only apologise – I have made my selection based on their ability, as a whole, to tell the story of Cheshire's parks and gardens, and I hope that you enjoy reading this story as much as I have enjoyed telling it.

Top: Thornton Manor is glimpsed through the forum.
Inset: Detail from the balustrade at Crewe Hall.

The earliest garden that we will look at here is that at Gawsworth Old Hall, which is now buried under the earth of several centuries but must have made a fine show when it was built in the seventeenth century. At this time, the style was for gardens to be formal and compartmentalised, usually using geometric patterns created from clipped foliage and grass or gravel paths. Such designs tended to be enclosed within walls and often great effort went into shaping the terrain into terraces and mounds. Additional decoration was provided by features such as statuary, garden buildings, pools and canals. With time, it became desirable to accompany gardens with wooded parks in which the formality was continued with straight walks and avenues, such as the one that still exists at Dunham Massey. Then, increasingly, woodland was treated as a 'Wilderness', in which a lightly planted area had naturalistic walks wending through it with features such as temples and statues carefully placed amongst the trees. The remains of such a Wilderness still cling to survival at Adlington Hall.

Formal gardens are rare in Great Britain today and so are treasured by garden historians even when only a trace of them remains. This is largely due to the eighteenth-century popularity of the landscape park, in which formality was swept away in favour of an imitation, or perfection, of nature with rural scenes of serpentine lakes, clumps of trees, and grass grazed by sheep coming almost directly up to the house. Busy exponents of this style in Cheshire were William Emes, John Webb, and the famous Humphry Repton, with their skills being used at Tatton Park, and Rode and Crewe halls.

By the Victorian period, an element of formality was creeping back in with elaborate showy gardens once more being created, usually near the main building, to create a colourful decorative ribbon between house and park. During this time, a designer who found a great deal of work in Cheshire was William Andrews Nesfield, who is most known for producing ornate parterres with swirling patterns in grass or gravel, planted with bright flowers, probably overlooking an earlier park. A famous example of Nesfield's work was enjoyed at Crewe Hall, although this, like most, was lost in the twentieth century. This era also saw the rise of public parks, an integral part of today's urban fabric that we cannot imagine being without. That designed by Joseph Paxton at Birkenhead was a world leader whilst those designed by his colleague Edward Kemp at Crewe and Chester are also fine examples.

An influx of plants from all over the Empire expanded the gardener's palette and Ness Botanic Gardens on the Wirral is in many ways an unsung hero of this movement in the early twentieth century. Its plant-mad founder funded many of the adventurers who supplied the horticultural lovelies that we now rely upon in our own gardens.

Rising at the same time was an approach to garden design that has come to represent the 'English' taste in many eyes – Arts and Crafts. This style combined formality with cosy informality and is represented in Cheshire by the fine work of Thomas Mawson, who designed Thornton Manor for Lord Leverhulme, and also advised at Tirley Garth.

I hope that by looking at such gardens in Cheshire I will be able not only to share my admiration of these places, but also spread an enthusiasm for garden history in a broader sense. This is not intended as a guidebook, as not all of the sites are regularly open to the public, but I do hope that this romp through Cheshire's historic parks and gardens will encourage the reader to travel at least through time to enjoy the gardens of the past.

Now down to practicalities: please allow me a few paragraphs to thank those people without whom this book would be just an itch in my typing fingers. The owners, gardeners, and staff of those parks and gardens described in these pages have all been generous in their support and time. Also invaluable have been the facilities and staff at various libraries who too often get taken for granted, in particular the British Library, the John Rylands Library, the Westminster Reference Library and the Cheshire Record Office. Other people to have most graciously given of their advice and knowledge are members of the Cheshire Society for Landscape History, Paul Everson, Peter de Figueiredo, Kath Gibson, Gavin Hunter, Maggie and Mike Taylor and Richard Turner. Thanks must also go to Gillian Mawrey, for rescuing me from an inconceivable life without garden history! Most important has been the support of my family and in particular the encouragement of Rosemary, John, Adam, Dorothy and Betty (definitely the most welcoming gardener in Cheshire). Last but never least, thank you to chauffeur, photographer, and lovely husband, Richard.

Above: Joan of Eaton stands in the Italian garden at Eaton Hall, Chester.
Below: A cast iron mastiff statue guards the forecourt of Dorfold Hall, Nantwich.

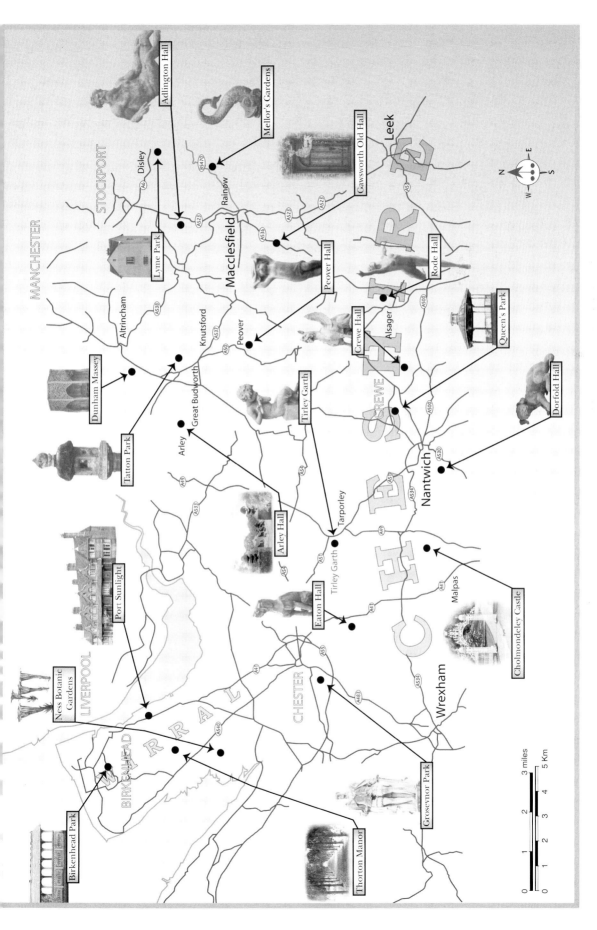

Gawsworth Old Hall, Macclesfield

*T*he dominant garden style in Britain today is that of the landscape park, in which swathes of undulating grass are decorated with lakes, clumps of trees, and grazing sheep or cows in a perfection of nature. This style has only been with us since the eighteenth century however, and before that gardens were very different indeed. Sixteenth- and seventeenth-century pleasure gardens were very formal and much more intricate, usually enclosed within walls that created a private paradise away from the outside world. Inside, they were split into compartments to create a network of garden areas through which to stroll and be entertained. These gardens would typically be planted with patterns of box and yew and some flowering plants for colour. There might be water features, ornamental buildings, statues, and complex ground levelling to create terraces, mounts and walkways, from which to view the scene.

Little remains of this style however, because the ensuing landscape movement was so popular as to sweep the country, leaving little of what was there before. As a result, such gardens have become something of an enigma and, for many, still remain one of the more distant, untouchable aspects of garden history. Whilst examples of Arts and Crafts gardens, Victorian design, and landscape parks are plentiful, the earlier garden feels very much an absent friend. Gawsworth, near Macclesfield, is therefore a real treasure, its value far greater than the immediate interest it holds for the garden lover simply looking for a pretty scene.

Gawsworth Old Hall is approached from the north-west down a narrow, tree-lined lane, which passes to the left Gawsworth New Hall. First time visitors often mistake this for the object of their trip because it is very grand, having

Top: The pretty floral garden to the west side of Gawsworth Old Hall.

The wall surrounding Gawsworth Old Hall is just low enough to allow a view of the nearby hills.

A little wooden door links Gawsworth Old Hall to St James' Church.

Gawsworth's current garden is bright & colourful.

The viewing mound behind the Old Hall gives a clue to what lies under the turf.

been built but never finished at the beginning of the eighteenth century to replace the Old Hall. By contrast, the original hall is delightfully 'Olde Englande' in appearance; its black and white timbered structure would not look out of place on a chocolate box, and parts of it even date back to medieval times.[1] It is first seen across one of a chain of decorative fishponds, with the neighbouring St James' Church adding to the restful scene. To the west of the Hall is a small but pleasant garden with rose beds and sunken lawn. To the uninitiated, this is the most attractive area of the Gawsworth grounds today but, in fact, it was given its present look as recently as the 1960s. Rather, Gawsworth's real attraction for us is to the back of the house, beneath what looks like a good-sized but rather rough walled field. This field is in fact the site of a formal seventeenth- or early eighteenth-century garden, the skeleton of which still lies buried under grass.

Today, Gawsworth is home to Timothy and Elizabeth Richards, who have become proficient at hosting successful public events there, ranging from concerts and theatre to vintage car rallies. They inherited the Old Hall from Monica and Raymond Richards, who moved there in 1962, subsequently carrying out significant restoration work on the building. Raymond Richards was a Cheshire historian previously living at the Gawsworth Old Rectory and acquiring the Old Hall from its owner, the 11th Earl of Harrington, when he decided to move to Ireland. Although usually tenanted, it had been in the hands of the Harrington family since having been bought by the 1st Earl of Harrington in 1725.[2] He bought it following the death of Lady Mohun, who held it after Lord Mohun was killed in 1712 in a famous duel with the 4th Duke of Hamilton, in which both combatants were killed. The duel was in fact fought over the issue of ownership of Gawsworth because Lord Mohun had inher-

ited it as a descendant of Charles Gerard (Earl of Macclesfield), who, in 1663 succeeded his uncle Edward Fitton V, who had died twenty years earlier. This succession had however been a controversial one and the 1712 duel had come about as the result of a long-running argument causing the Duke of Hamilton to feel that he was the rightful owner of Gawsworth.[3] Edward Fitton V had been the last of a line of Fittons to own Gawsworth, including his grandfather Edward III (1550-1606) who was a friend of Sir Walter Raleigh.[4]

The history of Gawsworth's ownership is difficult to untangle, and so too is that of its once magnificent landscape. Experts are divided on the dating of the garden, with Richard Turner, previously Archaeologist with Cheshire County Council, thinking it dates from around 1603 as a splendid and complete garden from that time, but others, including Paul Everson of English Heritage, feeling it is more likely to date from around 1680 or even later. It is possible that it was created in the early seventeenth century by the Fittons, as Edward Fitton III's daughter Mary was a great success at court, until an unfortunate pregnancy scandal, giving him hope that Queen Elizabeth would pay a visit. It is also possible that it was created later by Lord Mohun, perhaps being the legacy of his ambitious unfinished works to replace the old residence with the New Hall.[5] As Richard Turner says, 'there is more to discover at Gawsworth and it may even prove to have parts from all three of these periods'.[6] In the meantime though, we can enjoy the speculation!

The focus of these questions is the area to the south of the house which is the size of several football pitches. It is almost square and is still surrounded by a red brick wall which is straight apart from the southern boundary, where it curves out into an arc. The western stretch is exactly 300 yards long, and as such is one of the first clues that this area did not

Opposite page: Gawsworth's 'Rookery' terrace & St James' Church are best admired from across one of the tranquil fishponds.

simply evolve as need dictated. Rather, it was very carefully designed. Documentary evidence on Gawsworth from that period is lacking, so interpretation of the site has relied upon the visual evidence represented by the 'lumps and bumps' still showing through the grass. For many years experts such as the great nineteenth-century Cheshire historian George Ormerod had believed that the mysteriously sculpted ground at Gawsworth represented what had been a Tudor 'tilting ground', the site of jousts and other sporting tournaments: 'On the side of the grounds nearest the church is a long and lofty terrace, commanding an extensive prospect, in which the broken end of the Cloud is a most conspicuous object, and terminating in a large platform, in which is hollowed an irregular crescent, traditionally said to have been used for the exhibitions of wrestling and other rural sports by the Fittons.'[7] In the 1980s, Richard Turner carried out several archaeological surveys of Gawsworth, which have provided the layman with a tremendous insight into the past, although not enough to date it with certainty. As Paul Everson says, 'the garden remains at Gawsworth are absolutely stunning as an archaeological complex encompassing earthworks, buildings, planted material and topographical aspects like axes of approach … Dr Turner did everyone a service by giving it the attention he did, and opening up a discussion.'[8]

Today the garden is one huge grassed area with little to hold the interest of the uniniti- ated but originally it would have been divided into many separate areas, like the 'garden rooms' style which is currently popular. At the south western corner of the walled area is a mound of earth, which once had a matching twin at the south eastern corner, although this is now rather flat due to its sand having been removed during the Second World War. Originally though, this would have been used to survey the garden as a whole, its shapes and patterns being best viewed from above.

Another opportunity to view the garden is given by a raised walk which runs alongside the western wall and is mirrored by a similar walk on the eastern side. It is tall enough to also give a view over the wall, the top of which sits just below the scene of the distant hills of Beeston, Peckforton, Wales and even the Pennines. The walk begins at a fishpond beyond the house to the north, where a door cuts through the wall to the churchyard of St James', and then passes the 'Rookery', which is a terrace planted with lime trees. These limes are of varying ages but those in the corners are ancient and are believed to have been part of a formal pattern of trees. According to Richard Turner, this area was separated from the house and the rest of the garden by a tall brick wall. This reflects its use as an enclosed and secluded space which would offer privacy from anyone in the rest of the garden, except for those on the walk above. The southern end of this area is slightly raised and so Turner suggests it may have been used as either a bowling green or as a spot to erect marquees.[9]

Continuing south beyond the terrace is a rectangular sunken area which Turner's archaeology has shown to have been shaped by sculpting red clay. This is entered by descending three steps from the north or west and one from the south, and to the east it opens up directly into the rest of the garden. The northern steps

were then retained by brick walls, behind which may have been flowerbeds and turfed walks. The western steps were not retained by walls and so would have been more gently sloping but there is evidence that they would have been planted with regular lines of trees. It is probable that these were clipped yew or box in the style of the day. These steps would have provided a pleasant stroll and would probably have overlooked some kind of formal knot garden in their centre.

A canal with a circular pond at its end in the popular thermometer shape ran down the centre of the whole garden, pointing from north to south towards the arc in the wall. Today only a dribble of the canal survives, with a rough line of trees which may well have been part of a formal hedge.

It takes a strong imagination to look at the lumps and bumps of the garden at Gawsworth today and appreciate what it once would have been. The visitor yearns to see it through the eyes of the Fittons, but owner Timothy Richards is adamant that the hand of restoration will not be felt here because 'once you've dug up earthworks you've then got a major problem maintaining them – you've dug a rod for your own back'.

Richards' interest in Gawsworth is in many ways tied to its role in social history, reflected in his decision to preserve rather than recreate the garden, which tends as a result to be rather overlooked, with visitors enjoying the house instead. What he has continued however is the tradition of theatrical hospitality present all those centuries ago. Its showy gardens would have made Gawsworth an important social centre in the northwest and Richards' aim is to continue this role, still attracting Manchester folk to Gawsworth to enjoy the open-air theatre. This keeps Gawsworth a familiar name and destination across the county, as it would have been centuries ago.

And the eccentric streak of Gawsworth's earlier owners has been continued too: the scandal of illegitimate pregnancies and fatal duels is a thing of the past, but ebullient Timothy Richards creates something of a stir by throwing himself into his role as host. He revels in the theatricality of Gawsworth's theatre days, opening the gates and inspecting picnics with great aplomb, often mounting the stage to present fortunate performers with a bar of 'Gawsworth chocolate'. This is not however merely a sign of a quirky personality, but also of a shrewd business mind, as he must realise that in today's world a heritage property's residents are just as much a marketing tool as its fine furniture. To speak of such commercial things as marketing may seem horribly crude when describing such a unique place, but it is a harsh reality that historic properties cost a

fortune to maintain and without the backing of a huge organisation such as the National Trust, they simply cannot support themselves by dint of entry ticket alone, especially when their most valuable asset is buried beneath turf. On a good summer day, Gawsworth may take £100 from heritage visitors and, as Richards says, this will not even cover the cost of replacing the carpets they walk over. If this day is ended by an open-air performance however, the day's takings may be substantially nearer the amount needed to keep it in good working order. Yet although a property must be run with a determined business mind rather than dewy-eye to the past, Richards manages to combine this with a genuine feel for Gawsworth's historic spirit of displaying its treasures. As he says, 'opening one's house is a very ancient custom where you would share your gardens with the public'.

Inset opposite: Timothy & Elizabeth Richards keep Gawsworth Old Hall looking cheerful.
Below: Gawsworth is full of shady corners, including its fishponds.

Above: Gawsworth's original garden, with its mounds, terraces & varied walks, now lies under grassy turf. Below: The view from the mound shows how the garden wall stretches out in a perfect arc.

Above: The west corner of Gawsworth Old Hall.

Select Bibliography

de Figueiredo, Peter and Treuherz, Julian. *Cheshire County Houses*. Phillimore, Sussex, 1988.
English Heritage Register of Parks and Gardens of Special Historic Interest, 1999.
Ormerod, George. *The History of the County Palatine and City of Chester*, Volume 3. Lackington, Hughes, Harding, Mavor, and Jones, London, 1819.
Richards, Raymond. *Gawsworth Hall, Cheshire*. Heritage House Group Ltd, Derby, 2001.
Strong, Roy. *The Renaissance Garden in England*. Thames and Hudson, London, 1979, paperback edition reprint 1998.

References

1   *English Heritage Register of Parks and Gardens of Special Historic Interest*, 1999.
2   Raymond Richards, *Gawsworth Hall, Cheshire*, 2001, p35.
3   *English Heritage Register of Parks and Gardens of Special Historic Interest*, 1999.
4   George Ormerod, *The History of the County Palatine and City of Chester*, Volume 3, 1819, p166.
5   Paul Everson, email to Linden Groves, 26th August 2003.
6   Richard Turner, email to Linden Groves, 15th August 2003.
7   George Ormerod, *The History of the County Palatine and City of Chester*, Volume 3, 1819, p293.
8   Paul Everson, email to Linden Groves, 26th August 2003.
9   Richard Turner, *Gawsworth Hall Gardens: A History and Guide to the Great Elizabethan Garden at Gawsworth, Cheshire*, 1990, p13.

Cholmondeley Castle, Malpas

The setting of Cholmondeley Castle is sublimely romantic, resting on a hill where it can watch over the slopes of its garden to the park beyond, and so seems like the natural spot for such a building. In fact though, it has not always been so, as when the Cholmondeley family first lived at this estate in the twelfth century,[1] the house was a half-timber manor in the lower part of today's park, where the family chapel still stands. The family was rising socially however, reflected in Hugh Cholmondeley being made an Earl in 1706. In addition Hugh Cholmondeley invested great energy in creating what must have been impressive gardens around this house, on which he later undertook various rebuilding work.[2] At the time, there was great importance placed on orchards and kitchen gardens to provide food, but pleasure gardens would also be made, as the source of entertainment and prestige. The style of the day was for formal pleasure gardens with long, straight alleys created from clipped yew and box, ornate parterres, smart water features such as canals and pools, and plenty of embellishments in the form of gateways, buildings and statuary. The Earl of Cholmondeley's gardens would have been fine examples of this style as they were laid out by George London, who had already worked on many important properties in England including Hampton Court Palace's Privy Garden and Wilderness.

The Article of Agreement which was drawn up in 1695 between London and the Earl is now held at the Cheshire Record Office in Chester and shows that London was paid £350 'for the making of one piece of ground on the South side of Cholmley Hall into a fruit plantation and

Top: The current 'castle' is a fairytale concoction.
Above inset: Silver Garden statue.

*In early summer,
Cholmondeley's glades are
full of romance.*

*The focus of the Temple Garden
is a warrior sheltering in an
island temple.*

*The castle looks out across the
well-clipped east terrace.*

*Below: Rhododendrons & azaleas are massed in the
western corner of the Temple Garden.*

though it has now taken a more natural look as it has become subsumed into the landscape. In the same bundle, and also not signed, dated or titled, is what must surely be a plan of one of the garden parterres. This amazingly intricate design has eight circular beds of flowers or gravel which are linked by curving lines of topiary to an eight-pointed star, also planted or gravelled, with the whole forming the shape of a lozenge.

London was not the only 'name' to be connected with the 1st Earl's gardens. Another contributor to both Hampton Court and the Cholmondeley gardens was Jean Tijou, a Huguenot refugee whose ornate ironwork was greatly admired, with the 'Tijou screen' at Hampton Court still standing today. For Cholmondeley he produced a big iron entrance gate that was subsequently removed by the 4th Earl to Houghton Hall in Norfolk. In 1797 he had inherited the hall down the female line from the Walpole family, of which the famous garden creator and commentator Horace Walpole was a member. Tijou had a Staffordshire-born apprentice, Robert Bakewell, who also went on to become celebrated for his ironwork, and he too worked at Cholmondeley, being employed to produce, amongst other things, bannisters for the house. These were later re-used and today stand in the castle.[5] In addition, John van Nost, a leading Flemish sculptor with a London studio, was commissioned to make a fountain, complete with stop clocks to control the water flow.[6] Other features included a bowling-green, the 'mowing' and 'rowling' of which, together with the walks, was the duty of gardener William Downes.[7] Downes was also responsible for looking after swans and an aviary of birds, and bore the burden that 'if a dammage happin to be done in the Grottoes or buildings in the gardens by the labourers or any other disorderly people' he would 'make good that same att his own cost'.[8] The gardens of today's Cholmondeley are superb, but it is impossible not to wish that we could see the earlier ones as well.

Instead, these gardens were submerged when

other divisions including making walks and alleys, and a 4ft deep Canal'.[3] With Henry Wise, London owned the famous Brompton Nursery in Kensington, which supplied plants to most of the great English garden-owners but, nevertheless, the Agreement is clear that the Earl himself was to supply the necessary trees, shrubs, and plants.

The Agreement also shows that some of the walks were to be turf and some gravel, whilst other documents at the Record Office give still more clues as to what the garden may have looked like. In a bundle of miscellaneous papers from this period is an unsigned, untitled, undated page on which is drawn a thermometer or key-shaped outline.[4] As this was the fashionable shape for lakes or canals at this time, we can conclude that this is a plan of the '4ft deep Canal' mentioned in the Article of Agreement. This canal still exists and its distinctive form can be made out in the park, al-

William Emes was brought in to modernise the property by the 4th Earl, who had been made Marquess of Cholmondeley. Emes was a landscape gardener very much in the style of 'Capability' Brown but seems to have been much more active in Cheshire than his more famous contemporary; perhaps Brown did not like to undertake work in this area. Emes worked at several Cheshire estates, including Tatton and at a site today associated more with sport than with nature, Oulton Park. This is now a busy motor-racing circuit but was designed by Emes for Philip Egerton in 1770,[9] and still today the cars scream past a landscaped lake and carefully positioned trees, as well as, even more surreally, past rather grand arches and monuments. At Cholmondeley, Emes buried London's work under a landscape park, just as happened at hundreds of estates across the country. Thus, centuries of fine garden design were lost under a carpet of grass and scattered with lakes and trees.

Of course, this new style of garden was also an important era of design in its own right. An estimate for work at Cholmondeley which was put together by William Emes in December 1777 shows the intention to plant hundreds of beech, oak, Spanish chestnuts, sycamore and Scotch Fir, all to be supplied at two feet tall (with the exception of the Scotch Fir which were one foot) after the Earl apparently disagreed with Emes' original proposal to supply them at eighteen inches.[10] Perhaps he was an impatient man! It is possible that some of the many trees planted by Emes are amongst those now forming woodland on the slopes to the west of the main hall, which are known as Castle or Tower Hill. This area had become overgrown but recently considerable energy has been invested into clearing it to create a pleasant (if strenuous!) woodland walk through sun-dappled rhododendrons, azaleas and bluebells. New trees were added to those of Emes, with funding help from the Countryside Commission. The view from the top of this hill of the undulating countryside of southern Cheshire

Opposite page inset: The southern terrace is split into garden rooms.
Below: A curving walk leads around the Temple Garden lake.

is so picturesque that it seems as though there may be an oil painting hung in front of a 'real' view – the natural impulse is to reach out to try to touch the scene.

With a sense of priorities that will appeal to many, it was only after dealing with the landscape that the Marquess then turned his attention to the house, which had undergone various changes over the years, with several architects including John Vanbrugh having been involved.[11] However, after years of neglect under the profligate 3rd Earl, it was deemed to have deteriorated beyond repair and so it was decided to rebuild the house, this time on higher ground, presumably to avoid any future problems with the damp that had plagued it. This new building is the same Cholmondeley

Castle that stands today and is a fantastically fairy-tale concoction harking back to misty 'days of old'. This was no accidental nostalgia, as is shown by this 'General Direction' from Lord Cholmondeley to William Turner, a local architect employed for the job: 'It is intended that the new Hall shall in every Respect have the appearance of an old Gothic Castle, as much as possible consistent with neatness, and peremptorily to exclude both from without and within every thing that is new fashioned.'[12]

Top: The Bakewell gates shimmer beyond a glade. Middle: The meadow walk is resplendent with bluebells. Bottom: An enticing path leads towards Tower Hill.

Trees were cleared in order that the scene of the Park and beyond could be enjoyed to its full potential, and as today's visitor admires the view south-east from the castle to two stretches of water, Deer Park Mere and Chapel Mere, he cannot but feel that this decision was a good one.[13] For the gardens, the Earl employed John Webb, a student of William Emes who became prolific in the north of England, and it is probably he who designed the terrace immediately around the house, as well as a lawn planted with specimen trees on the slope.[14] The terraces are relatively narrow, which from the outside creates the striking effect of the Castle being only perched on its hill, ready at any moment to topple into the gardens and then down into the park. From within however, the southern terrace has a surprisingly enclosed feel, being surrounded by a mossy, weathered stone wall. Whilst the structure of these terraces is old, they have now been developed into a series of garden rooms. The first is a yew-hedged compartment containing a swimming pool and brick pavilion pool house which was

built in the 1970s but re-uses some Bakewell ironwork. Next to this, with views over a sloping 'croquet lawn', is the lily pond garden in which a neat pool, hand dug in the 1980s, rests in an area planted with roses, irises and *Magnolia grandiflora*, Lady Cholmondeley's favourite. This area leads to the Silver Garden, so called after Queen Elizabeth II's Silver Jubilee. Here, Bakewell stair railings are re-used and wisteria clambers up the arched windows of the hall, creating an intimate, private area. The terrace to the east of the hall is laid out with an immaculate but daisy-spattered lawn and simple borders. On the slope below is a meadow walk where long grass is scattered with wildflowers such as buttercups, daffodils and bluebells, which spread like wildfire at Cholmondeley. This is reached from the house by a flight of steps that once led to a Cherry Walk, but sadly over the past twenty years all but one of the cherry trees have died of honey fungus.

Created in the early days of the castle was the Temple Garden, which remains one of Cholmondeley's greatest features. This was described in an 1894 issue of the *Gardener's Chronicle*: 'There is usually an element of incongruousness when a modern flower-garden with its flower-carpet beds and trim lawns are placed in the immediate vicinity of a mediaeval stronghold. In the view presented this defect is averted by placing the flower-garden on pleasantly-undulated land, at some distance from the Castle, and separated from it by groups and belts of trees and shrubs, which screen, but do not quite hide it from view. This portion is known as the Temple garden, from a temple which surmounts a mound in the centre, and was formed by the first Marquis for his daughter, afterwards Lady Charlotte

Top: Head Gardener Bill Brayford is a great admirer of Enkianthus.
Middle: The Bakewell railings are a fine sight in the Silver Garden.
Bottom: The modern Lily Pond Garden provides a pretty scene.

Bakewell gates welcome the visitors to Cholmondeley Castle.

Seymour. A laurel bank encircles the garden, and some fine specimens of Cupressus macrocarpa may be seen in the middle distance.'[15]

A third period of garden activity came in the 1950s and '60s with the arrival of Lavinia Cholmondeley, wife of the 6th Marquess, Hugh, who died in 1990. Lady Cholmondeley describes the garden on her arrival as being pleasant but too bereft of plants for her liking, as it boasted splendid trees but only a few specimen shrubs. She started on what became a lifetime's work to create something more to her taste, with early projects including the creation of a rose garden. In front of here today is a pretty walk bordered with weeping pear trees and beds of fabulous tulips, although these struggle against the mice who treat their bulbs as delicacies. In her own words, she never carried out any major garden projects in comparision to those of the past, but certainly there has been intensive replanting and rearranging including that on the terraces, with recent work seeing the creation of two beds of ornamental grasses on the 'croquet lawn' near the house.

By the time Lady Cholmondeley came to the Castle, the Temple Garden, which is set around a sunken lake, with shrubs and trees on its sloping banks, had by all accounts become virtually overgrown with rampant laurels and rhododendrons. Work began apace to clear it and Lady Cholmondeley laughingly tells of how guests were handed tools and told to knuckle down to work. The unfortunate guests, whoever they were, certainly did a good job; today the Temple Garden is once more the jewel in Cholmondeley's crown. An antique tone is here set by the astute recycling of features from the Old Hall, which is rather a theme at Cholmondeley. The entrances are through a set of eighteenth century pillars, or through a less grand sandstone gateway with ironwork thought to have been that designed by Jean Tijou for London's garden.[16] The square classical stone temple came originally from the Old Hall and stands proud on an island in a lilied lake, albeit obscured from some angles by an errant conifer. From between its pillars a warrior-figure watches over Lady Cholmondeley's koi carp. The curved lake is edged with pampas grass and juicy gunnera and the trim grass of its banks is decorated with two groups of lead cherubs, ornamental cherry trees, and also mature rhododendrons and azaleas in fiery shades. These are amassed to particularly spectacular effect, creating a rainbow reflection in the western corner of the lake, where alpines and bulbs are also planted, below a modern but complementary circular temple. The lake here is capped by a low bridge built of four stone dolphins, that originally formed a fountain but now have features softened with age.

A short stroll from the Temple Garden are gentler, pretty areas which have been planted into charming glades with daffodils, magnolias, and what Head Gardener Bill Brayford claims to be 'the best handkerchief tree in the country'. Visitors to the Cholmondeley gardens are greeted by this tranquil scene, where a captivating fairy-tale atmosphere is created by the Bakewell gate and screen straddling the drive. These were moved here in 1801, having once formed an entrance to the Old Hall but, now painted a romantic white, they look rather as though they have been brought from another world altogether. Passing through them on a sunny day, it is as though entering a magical kingdom …

Above: The Temple Garden is framed by many fine trees. Below: A modern bridge with a traditional rustic look leads to the Temple Garden island.

Above: The Temple Garden is well-admired from the western corner.
Below: Gunnera come to life in the Temple Garden.

Above: Stairs lead from the Cherry Walk to the east terrace.
Below: The castle enjoys wonderful park views across the meadow walk.

Select Bibliography

Cholmondeley, Lady. *Cholmondeley Castle Gardens*. Jarrold Publishing, 2002.
de Figueiredo, Peter and Treuherz, Julian. *Cheshire County Houses*. Phillimore, Sussex, 1988.
English Heritage Register of Parks and Gardens of Special Historic Interest, 1999.
Gardener's Chronicle, 12th May 1894, p589.
Hellyer, Arthur. 'New Intimacy and Old Plantings'. *Country Life*, Volume 166, 29th November 1979, p2000-3.
Jackson-Stops, Gervase. 'Cholmondeley Castle, Cheshire - I'. *Country Life*, Volume 154, 19th July 1973, p154-7.
Jackson-Stops, Gervase. 'Cholmondeley Castle, Cheshire - II'. *Country Life*, Volume 154, 26th July 1973, p226-30.
Lacey, Stephen. 'Unforgettable fire'. *Telegraph Magazine*, 6th November 2002, p50-55.
Ormerod, George. *The History of the County Palatine and City of Chester*, Volume 2. Lackington, Hughes, Harding, Mavor, and Jones, London, 1819.

The archive material used is held at the Cheshire Record Office (Cholmondeley Papers).

References

1   Lady Cholmondeley, *Cholmondeley Castle Gardens*, 2002, p15.
2   *English Heritage Register of Parks and Gardens of Special Historic Interest*, 1999.
3   Cholmondeley Papers DCH/A242.
4   Cholmondeley Papers DCH/x/17.
5   Cholmondeley Papers DCH/6/47.
6   Cholmondeley Papers DCH 16/47.
7   Cholmondeley Papers DCH/A248.
8   Cholmondeley Papers DCH/A248.
9   K M Goodway, *'William Emes - Landscape Gardener'* 14th May 1984. Manuscript in Cheshire Record Office SF/920EME/01.
10 Cholmondeley Papers DCH/A397.
11 *English Heritage Register of Parks and Gardens of Special Historic Interest*, 1999.
12 Cholmondeley Papers DCH/x/20, Sept 22nd 1801.
13 Cholmondeley Papers DCH/x/20.
14 *English Heritage Register of Parks and Gardens of Special Historic Interest*, 1999.
15 *Gardener's Chronicle*, 12th May 1894, p589.
16 *English Heritage Register of Parks and Gardens of Special Historic Interest*, 1999.

Dunham Massey, Altrincham

Dunham Massey was the home of a Saxon lord until 1070 when, following the Norman invasion, it was given to a conquering knight called Hamo de Massey. It then passed through many generations of de Masseys (all of whom were apparently called Hamo) until 1453 when it was carried through the female line to a family by the name of Booth. After several generations of Booths, it is in the seventeenth century that we start to find records of a garden at Dunham Massey of considerable interest, if of limited size. In 1696 an aerial painting of the site from the south-east was carried out by Dutch painter Adrien van Diest and in 1697 an aerial drawing from the south-west was undertaken by Leonard Knyff and engraved by his frequent collaborator Johannes Kip. Between them, these works comprehensively recorded the garden that had been enjoyed by the generations of Booths most immediately preceding that time.

These aerial views show most notably a moat around the house with a mount to the north-west. The mount is terraced, appears to be around ten metres high, and has at the top a small pavilion-style building. Designed primarily to afford views over the garden and beyond, such mounts had become a standard garden feature by the seventeenth century, their praises sung in 1625 by the influential Francis Bacon in his essay 'Of Gardens': 'I wish also, in the very middle, a fair mount, with three ascents, and alleys, enough for four to walk abreast; which I would have to be perfect circles, without any bulwarks or embossments; and the whole mount to be thirty foot high.'[1]

The seventeenth-century painting shows the moat to encircle the house, being narrow and regulated to the south and east, and more of a natural lake shape to the north and west. Within the moat to the east and west are modest formal gardens, with a walled and formally planted garden to the east of the house, and a walled grassed parterre to the west. The entrance is to the south, where a small bridge crosses the moat to a walled grassed forecourt

Above: Dunham Massey's moat now only stretches round two sides of the house.

A rustic seat among Dunham's rare collection of late flowering deciduous azazeas.

Hosta Sigboldiana Elgans in the bog garden. Crocosmia Paniculata in flower at rear.

Cauteya Spicata 'Robusta' in the bog garden late summer.

Bird's eye view of Dunham Massey from north by John Harris, c 1750 (Dunham Massey, The Stamford Collection, The National Trust Photographic Library/Angelo Hornak).

with cupolated turrets at the furthest corners from the house. Beyond these gardens is lightly planted parkland (which had already been recorded as early as 1362 in manorial accounts).[2]

It is thought that these gardens had been created by 'Old' Sir George Booth in the early seventeenth century. After his death in 1652, the estate passed to his grandson, 'Young' Sir George. Unfortunately, the Parliamentarian political activities of this Sir George and subsequently of his son Henry, the 1st Earl of Warrington, resulted in great financial difficulties and the virtual collapse of the Dunham Massey estate. The Schedule of the Debts of Henry Booth, the 1st Earl of Warrington, record the cost of his imprisonments: 'Three times Committed to the tower, my lying there and charg of my tryall may moderatly be rated at £2000.'[3]

It was not until the eventual succession in 1694 of the 2nd Earl of Warrington that work began to rectify the financial situation. It was this descendant of 'Old' Sir George, also called George, who commissioned van Diest and Kip and Knyff to record his ancestors' property. These commissions imply that the 2nd Earl must have been very proud of his estate at that time, but by no stretch of the imagination was it to stand still from this point. The seventeenth-century views are remarkably detailed but the visitor of today could not navigate his way around Dunham Massey using either the Kip and Knyff picture or that of Van Diest.

The 2nd Earl's priority on succeeding was to clear the family debts, which it is estimated had reached £50,000.[4] This was achieved chiefly through his unhappy marriage to Mary Oldbury, who brought a large dowry.[5] He also incorporated much land into the impressive park to the south of the house, planting a prodigious amount of trees, predominately oak, beech, lime and chestnut.[6] He must have been a shrewd man: today the park is a stunning landscape with peaceful acre upon acre of mature trees interspersed with grazing deer, but having seen the effects of financial difficulty, he planted it with a very practical eye to profit for future generations. Even when relatively

The south front of house looks out over mature wooded parkland.

Deer enjoy the shade of the pollared lime trees in the south front.

immature it was considerable and in 1762 it was recorded as having 31,246 trees within its walls, excluding hawthorns, elders and some alders.[7] The Earl's economic plan was to prove successful and from 1792 timber and bark sales regularly brought in over twenty per cent of the estate's income.[8] Early on in the park's development he created in it the South and South-East Avenues and this symbolises the ultimate gaining of control – not only was he able to nurture nature by planting the trees, he was then able to manipulate it by creating walks and avenues through the middle. These avenues, in such an extensive park, made an unmissable statement about his social standing. Whilst allowing access to the house for pedestrians, riders and carriages, they also created fantastically framed views out from the house, and in to the house for passers-by to marvel at.

Having stabilised Dunham Massey's fortunes, he then brought in little-known architect John Norris to refurbish the early seventeenth-century house, eventually encasing the old core in a more acceptable new shell. In the process he reconstructed the serene inner courtyard at the centre. In 1823 a covered passageway was constructed through this courtyard but it took on something like its present appearance when in the twentieth century the 9th Earl of Stamford brought in minor architect Joseph Compton Hall to refurbish the house once again, although the enchanting borders and fountain we enjoy today are largely the result of work by the National Trust.

The 2nd Earl must have had inexhaustible energy and drive because he continued to carry out a great deal of work on the grounds. We are fortunate that he commissioned four aerial paintings of Dunham Massey from John Harris the Younger in 1751. By comparing these paintings to those of van Diest and Kip and Knyff carried out at the start of his

occupancy, we can identify exactly what work went on under his ownership, between the earlier works and those of Harris.

From these Harris paintings, we can see that it was the 2nd Earl who largely gave Dunham Massey the shape we see today. Perhaps the most immediately noticeable difference to the gardens compared to the earlier views is the addition of an imposing stable block to the west of the forecourt where previously there had been another walled and ordered garden. The clock of the coach-house arch is dated as 1721, and it is through this arch that today's visitor enters Dunham Massey. The forecourt is no longer walled but instead has a pier with the figure of a lion at each of the southern corners with the park, and a stone pier with a flaming urn at each of the northern corners where the

Top: The Moss Garden is a surprising corner of Dunham Massey.
Middle: The house is framed by fine lawns. Bottom: Visitors enjoy resting in the quirky Root Arbour.

forecourt meets the house. There are three lines of tightly shaped trees on each side, running out to the park (these pollarded lime trees, *Tilia cordata*, were replanted at the end of the twentieth century). At the entrance to the house rests a sundial supported by a black slave made from lead, which can still be seen today, and is similar to one at Arley Hall.

The moat is by now no more than an L-shaped lake to the north and north-west of the house, and the mount is rather less angular and dominating. What was a large walled ornamental garden to the east of the house has been replaced by a much smaller walled area. Beyond this, stretching to the south-east and north beyond the moat, is formally planted woodland which surrounds regular lawns and stretches of water. A vista has been cut on the north axis, providing a far-reaching view from the house to an obelisk some 600 metres away in Whiteoaks Wood.

The park has become densely planted and the 2nd Earl has created more avenues, or allées, which fan out from the house in the impressive 'goose foot' style that had gained popularity in Italy and France at the beginning of the previous century. This 'goose foot' effect can still be enjoyed today and from west to east the avenues are: Langham Grove (at the end of which is an obelisk dated 1714), South Avenue, South-East Avenue, Charcoal Drive and Smithy Drive. In the Harris paintings there is a sixth avenue, now lost, that leads south-west to the river. The park wall was completed in 1751 and placed within it were park buildings, obelisks, and statues, although the 5th Earl was

Above: The orangery sits on a spendid lawn. Below: A parterre perches between the north front and the moat, planted with a central yucca with 'Diabolo' in bed edged with Salvia farinacea 'Victoria'.

to remove many of these in the late 1780s. Through the trees today there are still tantalising glimpses of both functional and ornamental park features: between Langham Grove and South Avenue is Old Man's Pool; in the southern corner of the park is open grassland called Ice House Plain on which there are the remains of a brick icehouse, although this area is used as a deer sanctuary with no public access; between South Avenue and Charcoal Drive is Island Pool; between the Main Drive and Charcoal Drive is an eighteenth-century slaughterhouse; and between Charcoal Drive and Smithy Drive is Smithy Pool and an eighteenth-century deer shelter.[9] Almost miraculously, the park is much as it was in the 2nd Earl's day, in spite of the loss of some of its built or water features. Any changes have tended to be because of woodland management or storm damage.

Observing the 2nd Earl's efforts in transforming the family's fortunes as well as its estate, we can easily be left rather in awe of him. It is touching therefore to stumble across an often overlooked but endearing aspect of an otherwise stately garden: a collection of dogs' graves which form a straight line down the noble northern vista. These simple but charming graves catalogue many generations of much-loved Dunham Massey dogs, beginning with the 2nd Earl's 'Puggs', whose stone is dated 1702.

From the 2nd Earl of Warrington the estate passed in 1758 to his daughter Mary and her husband the 4th Earl of Stamford, thus carrying the property from the Booth family to the Greys. Although essentially based at the principal Stamford residence of Enville in Staffordshire, they did manage to transform what was known by 1765 as the New Park, to the southeast of Dunham Massey, but which had previously been the Higher Park, dating back as far as the 'main' park. Mary clearly kept up to date with garden fashions and the work carried out was in the new landscape style, essentially with clumps of trees rather than avenues. We cannot be sure whether 'capability' Brown actually carried out the work here, but the 4th Earl did apparently recommend him for a royal appointment.[10] In spite of some building work around the edges, New Park was maintained as a park until being requisitioned in the Second World War when it was host to German prisoners of war. Following the war it became a golf course, with part being compulsorily bought for a covered reservoir, and it is now accessible only by public footpath.

After Mary's death in 1772 Dunham Massey passed to her son, the 5th Earl of Stamford. Like many of his gentlemanly contemporaries, he undertook the Grand Tour of Europe and returned to make several significant changes to the grounds of Dunham Massey.

Looking at the garden account books, there seems to have been little activity in the gardens for the first decades of his ownership. Purchases were mainly stock for the kitchen garden, such as the December 1797 purchase at a cost of nine shillings of 'Nine dwarf Cherry Trees to plant in the kitchen garden'.[11] The notes of the 5th Earl's son provide many fascinating insights into the gardens at this time. In August 1797 he records a terrible hailstorm in which stones of 2.25 inches in diameter caused 7,169 broken panes in hothouses, vineries and frames: the consequent expense must have been staggering.[12]

By October 1798 the account books show that the Earl's interest in his Dunham Massey gardens was aroused and William North, nurseryman, was paid £3 4s 6d for 'Trees, Plants to the Flower ground'.[13] By the nineteenth century commercial nurseries were common and accessible and it was using such means that the 5th Earl added huge numbers of plants to his gardens. The accounts record many purchases from nurserymen, one of the largest being on 11th June 1802 to 'Messrs. Grimswood and Wykes, Nursery Men at Kensington Gardens' for £39 9s 3d.[14] Putting this sum in the context of the nine shillings paid for the nine cherry trees only five years earlier, we can see just what a spectacular range of plants must have been supplied by Grimswood. Throughout the summer of 1802, and indeed for the next few years, we see a regular purchasing of horticultural delights, with many coming from the local company Carr & Caldwell.[15]

In accordance with the proliferation of plants in the garden was the steady rise in staff levels in the early nineteenth century. Regular annual activities of these staff included wasp destroying in June and leaf raking in the autumn, for which additional workers, mainly women, were brought in. By the end of the 5th Earl's ownership in 1822, the costs of leaf raking were not inconsiderable. A record of 30th November 1822 shows twenty-five women and men or boys to have been paid for 337.5 days of raking, at a rate of one shilling a day.[16]

Many of the new plants must have gone into the garden we see today to the east of the house with its memorable lawn and naturalistic plantings, for which the 5th Earl is largely responsible. This sweeping lawn is one of Dunham Massey's most famous features today but is not one that comes easily. The current Head Gardener, Graham Kendall, finds this deceptively simple feature to be the most labour-demanding part of his domain to look after, requiring twice-weekly trims for much of the growing season. The lawn is dominated by a stunning red brick orangery, which is thought to date from the second half of the eighteenth century. The compact but delightful orangery originally had a slate roof that was replaced with glass by the 7th Earl, and then restored to slate by the National Trust.

In December 1799 the garden account book records great purchasing and activity when a 'pine pit' was constructed for the growing of pineapples, to the cost of £313 2s 9d.[17] Only six months later this pit caused yet more expenditure when it needed £1 17s 8d worth of repairs by a bricksetter. Any produce supplied by this construction would have been very expensive indeed!

The account books also reveal an interesting detail of the routine of the Stamford family at this time. Throughout the early years of the nineteenth century, we see a pattern of boxes being sent from the Dunham Massey garden to Enville in March, to London from April to June, and to a residence called 'High Lake' in September. Presumably these were the chief times in which the family was absent from Dunham Massey. What the accounts do not of course show was the whereabouts of the family over the winter, when there would have been less produce to send out.

The 5th Earl also contributed many of the dogs' graves, including his Harlequin Great Dane by the name of Turpin, who died in 1783 having first been immortalised by Thomas Stringer in two matching portraits which hang today on either side of the mantelpiece in the Great Hall.

The 5th Earl died in 1819 and the 6th Earl's ownership seems to produce few surprises. He too added to the stock of the garden, although his horticultural shopping habit does not seem to reach the proportions of his father. Instead we find records of kitchen garden produce being sold from Dunham Massey for a profit.[18] Like many gentlemen of the age, the 6th Earl was a plant enthusiast and was a life governor and hereditary member of the Manchester Botanical and Horticultural Society, which had been founded in 1827 and had a botanic garden in Old Trafford, near the current home of the Manchester United football team.[19]

Amongst the many exotic plants introduced to Dunham Massey were two 'Lambertin pine' plants, or *Pinus lambertiana*, from California, apparently raised from seed, of which a note in the 6th Earl's own hand exists in the Dunham Massey Papers.[20] There are several such records of plants in these papers, including a list of vines.[21] Given the family's passion for new plants, it seems appropriate that today the National Trust pursues a policy of enriching the plantings within the historic structure of the garden. Thus, the twenty-first-century visitor to Dunham Massey is looking at contemporary planting designs within the historic lay-out. The wonderful range of plants mean that whenever Graham Kendall walks around the garden, his progress is often impeded by eager members of the public asking for help identifying unusual varieties.

Sadly, the 6th Earl's son, Lord Grey of Groby, died before his father so the Earldom passed straight to his son in 1845. In contrast to the respectability that had been dominant at Dunham Massey since the politics of the Booths, the 7th Earl heralds a return of scandal to the estate's history, marrying first the daughter of a bedmaker, and then a bare-backed circus rider. This couple's reception by the increasingly opulent Bowdon society was so frosty that they spent their time at Enville. For our purposes though, the 7th Earl had a great redeeming feature in that he was a keen gardener and left his mark on Dunham Massey in spite of his absence. He introduced fashionable Victorian island beds in front of the orangery, next to which he created a charming Root Arbour. The Root Arbour can today be found further north on the lawn, in front of a Well House that had been built in the early eighteenth-century for feeding water into the house.[22]

The 7th Earl did not have any children, so Dunham Massey was due to pass to his cousin, the 8th Earl. This Earl however also had his share of controversy as his third marriage, which resulted in children, was to the 'Hottentot' housekeeper he met in South Africa.[23] There was debate over the entitlement of the half-caste children and so when the 8th Earl died in 1890, having never owned Dunham Massey, it was arranged in the House of Lords that the estate would pass to his nephew.[24]

When the 9th Earl inherited in 1905, changes began once more. The Earl was determined to settle at Dunham Massey with his family, returning the Stamfords to residency. Work was carried out on the estate in preparation for their arrival and they officially returned to great welcome in 1906. Whilst admiration is stilted for the work done on the house at this time, life returned once more to the gardens. A lined pattern of paths was created in front of the orangery where a charming fountain pond plays today, and most of the island beds were removed.[25] In 1905 this Earl also created a geometric parterre with Golden Yew hedges within the moat on the north front. He also created a

rose garden beyond the moat. This was abandoned in the Second World War however and as the beech hedge around it grew out of control into a shady dell, the encroaching moss was encouraged until this now Zen-like area is one of the few moss gardens in the country. Having breathed new life into Dunham Massey, the 9th Earl died prematurely in 1910 from an infection picked up in Palestine and the estate passed to his son, the 10th Earl.

During the First World War Dunham Massey suffered as badly as the rest of the country's grand houses. All but one of the gardeners were called up to fight, the house served as a hospital, and attempts to turn the lawn to potatoes are not included in the canon of great garden movements seen at Dunham Massey! The Second World War only made the situation worse, and Head Gardener Mr Gillies struggled single-handedly with maintenance. It was not until the unmarried and reclusive 10th Earl of Stamford left Dunham Massey to the National Trust on his death in 1976 that its return to glory began.

So what layers of Dunham Massey's varied garden history remain today? The visitor approaches the house from the north-west alongside what is still a stunning moat. A few years ago, he might have caught sight of a terrapin, that spent a few seasons at Dunham Massey as an uninvited guest, before disappearing once more. A view can be glimpsed of the mount, although several generations of owners and the fashions they followed have conspired to reduce it to a flattened hillock dotted with laburnums and false acacias. Passing through the 2nd Earl's stable archway, he is then greeted by the eighteenth-century-style lines of lime trees, all leading out southwards from the house down the forecourt to the 2nd Earl's now mature park with its five remaining avenues, stretching as far as the eye can see. Passing across the south front of the house and round to the east, he then enters what is a pleasant wooded area, having been planted in the late twentieth century with a bog garden, hydrangeas, and an important collection of azaleas.

Above: Deer roam freely over Dunham Massey's park & south front.
Below: The entrance to the Moss Garden offers a glimpse of this intriguing nook.

An enjoyable stroll leads across a wooded ha-ha and stream to the great sweeping lawn of the 5th Earl, watched from across the moat by the rather austere house, fronted by the Edwardian parterre. On this lawn it is the eighteenth-century orangery that catches the eye but moving onwards, dainty stepping stones lead the visitor across the canal with its richly planted banks to the dogs' graves and north vista.

Thanks to its ability to 'deliver the goods' for all garden enthusiasts whether they enjoy exuberant plantings with a sweep of lawn, the mystery of an aged moat and mount, or the drama of an ancient park, Dunham Massey is known as a great and loved garden. Due to its care under the auspices of the National Trust, its future now seems secure as well. All in all, a veritable showpiece of prudent good taste and centuries of good management: the 2nd Earl (and his dog Puggs) would be proud.

The dogs' graves are in full view of the house.

Select Bibliography

English Heritage Register of Parks and Gardens of Special Historic Interest, 1999.

Bowdon History Society, comp. *Images of England: Bowdon and Dunham Massey*. Tempus Publishing, Gloucestershire, 1999.

Bacon, Francis. 'Of Gardens', *Essays*, 1625. JM Dent & Sons, London, 1906 edition, reprinted 1965.

Crosby, Alan. *A History of Cheshire*. Phillimore, West Sussex, 1996.

de Figueiredo, Peter and Treuherz, Julian, *Cheshire County Houses*. Phillimore, Sussex, 1988.

Harris, John. 'A Birds-Eye View of Dunham Massey'. *Apollo*, July 1978, p4-11.

Jackson-Stops, Gervase. 'Dunham Massey - I'. *Country Life*, 4th June 1981, p1562-4.

Jackson-Stops, Gervase. 'Dunham Massey - II'. *Country Life*, 11th June 1981, p1664-8.

Jackson-Stops, Gervase. 'Dunham Massey - III'. *Country Life*, 2th July 1981, p18-21.

Jackson-Stops, Gervase. 'Dunham Massey - IV'. *Country Life*, 9th July 1981, p106-9.

Laing, Alistair. 'Sensible, Sincere Creatures'. *Country Life*, 8th February 1990, p62-5.

Rothwell, James, *Dunham Massey*, National Trust Enterprises, London, 2000.

Sales, John. 'A Quality Unsurpassed'. *Country Life*, 9th June 1994 p112-5.

Shoemaker, Candice, ed. *Encyclopedia of Gardens: History and Design*. Fitzroy Dearborn, London, 2001.

The archive material used is held at the John Rylands Library (Dunham Massey Papers).

References

1   Francis Bacon. 'Of Gardens', *Essays*, 1625. 1906 edition, reprinted 1965, p140.
2   Dunham Massey Papers, Introduction, p32, or ref EGR2/1/2/1-2.
3   Dunham Massey Papers, EGR3/6/2/1/1.
4   Dunham Massey Papers, Introduction, p6.
5   Peter de Figueiredo, and Julian Treuherz. *Cheshire Country Houses*. 1988, p81.
6   James Rothwell, *Dunham Massey*, 2000, p48.
7   Following the calculations made by Reverend Dr Evans on 24th June 1762. EGR3/7/1/121.
8   James Rothwell. *Dunham Massey*. 2000, p49.
9   *English Heritage Register of Parks and Gardens of Special Historic Interest*, 1999.
10 James Rothwell. *Dunham Massey*. 2000, p50.
11 Dunham Massey Papers EGR 7/7/2.
12 Dunham Massey Papers EGR4/2/12/3.
13 Dunham Massey Papers EGR7/7/2.
14 Dunham Massey Papers EGR 7/7/2.
15 Dunham Massey Papers EGR 7/7/2 and 7/7/3.
16 Dunham Massey Papers EGR 7/12/12.
17 Dunham Massey Papers EGR7/7/1.
18 Dunham Massey Papers EGR7/7/5.
19 Dunham Massey Papers EGR4/2/10/20.
20 Dunham Massey Papers, Catalogue, p74, EGR7/19/5/7.
21 Dunham Massey Papers EGR7/19/5/8.
22 James Rothwell. *Dunham Massey*. 2000, p44.
23 James Rothwell. *Dunham Massey*. 2000, p62.
24 Gervase Jackson-Stops. 'Dunham Massey'. *Country Life*, 9th July 1981 p106.
25 James Rothwell. *Dunham Massey*. 2000, p44.

Adlington Hall, Macclesfield

U nusually for an age where so many of our historic properties are frozen in time as impressive examples of the fine taste and excellent design of the past, Adlington Hall is still evolving according to the preferences of the Legh family, branches of which have owned it since the fourteenth century.[1] At that time it was a simple hunting lodge, but in the fifteenth and sixteenth centuries it evolved into a black and white timbered structure of the type so beloved of Cheshire. This style can still be seen in the east front, but in the seventeenth-century a brick north front was added, absorbing the earlier Great Hall. In the eighteenth-century the property passed to Charles Legh who impressed the stamp of his age, adding a brick west front and also a rather grand south front with Ionic portico. Thus the Hall evolved into a quadrangle, with each side exhibiting a different period of Cheshire style.

By all accounts, Charles Legh was a man with many enthusiasms, and as no records exist of an architect having been employed at Adlington, he may have had a major hand in the design of his additions to the house.[2] He also invested a great deal of energy in the Hall's surrounds, laying out gardens which at least in part still exist today.

To the north of the house, where there is now a new rose garden, was a rectangular formal pool, surrounded by light woodland. A pleasant walk stretched around this pool, and was clearly well-used, as one of several eighteenth-century paintings attributed to Thomas Bardwell shows the walk being used to exercise quite a collection of pet dogs.[3] Today this area is reached by crossing the empty bed of a moat and walking up a wide cobbled path, perhaps once a cascade.

It is probable that the walled kitchen garden to the south of the house also dates from this period.[4] The primary purpose of this garden would have been the functional one of providing

Top: The Chinese Bridge now lacks its summerhouse.

A freshly planted knot garden to the east of the hall struggles against marauding rabbits.

Plants thrive in the new Father Tiber garden

Father Tiber watches over his new garden surroundings.

A cobbled pathway leads to a popular new rose garden.

food for the house and the north wall was set up to be heated to enable the production of vegetables and fruit such as peaches and apricots. Nevertheless, efforts were made to ensure that it was an attractive addition to Adlington, with crenellated tops to the walls.

The south front is resolutely unromantic, with a large open front centred on a plain grass turning circle in the eighteenth-century style. From here however, iron gates dated 1688 announce a beautiful old lime avenue and by the time the visitor has walked the length of this, he is in the mood for something special. This is certainly provided by a toy cottage, the Shell House, so called because the inside is decorated with shells and coloured mirrors. This diminutive brick building still exists in good condition and is a real delight. The façade is formed into a triangle and looks forwards to a Yew Walk. Around the back and side is a rockery, which was extended in recent years but is thought to be from the early nineteenth century when such features were very popular, inspired mainly by the increasing exploration of exotic mountainous regions. This rockery is constructed of surprisingly large boulders so it must have been quite a team of workmen who put it together. The back of the

Shell House looks out to a pleasure ground in the 'Wilderness' style so admired at the time, in which winding paths offered an opportunity to explore a mysteriously wooded area, which was often scattered with gimmicky, built features to add an extra element of excitement. Here, a collection of intriguing follies and bridges was scattered amongst the trees to provide 'events' in the woodland stroll.

One of the first buildings to be encountered in the Adlington Wilderness was the Tig House, a small square pavilion which overlooks the river Dene to one side and to the other a grassy glade which was used as a tennis court. The Tig House has a vaguely oriental appearance and as such is an early example of the Chinoiserie tradition in which a craze for a supposedly Chinese garden style was fueled by Sir William Temple's writing *Upon the Gardens of Epicurus* in 1685. In this, a Chinese form of garden was extolled, that is to say, it encouraged a scattered and disordered placing of features such as streams and pavilions, in a style that was seen to be Oriental but in fact represented at best the general spirit of such gardens rather than the detailed reality. Indeed, its funny name has probably evolved from 'T'ing house', a familiar Chinoiserie term.

Opposite page: Adlington's Hall is built around a courtyard.
Above: The east front is a traditional black & white timbered structure.

Continuing the loosely-oriental theme is the Chinese Bridge nearby to the south, which leads across the river Dene. In the centre of this brick bridge was a many-sided Chinese summerhouse, now lost, from which one could watch the river.

Also hiding amongst the trees was a statue of the river god Father Tiber, who rested on some rocks looking, appropriately, down a slope towards a pool and the Dene. Another god was represented at the far reaches of the Wilderness by the Temple of Diana, a circular domed temple with Doric columns and leafy carvings. From the edges of the Wilderness a distant 'castle' could be viewed in the park; in fact this was just a sham, built to draw the eye out into the distant view. Other features carefully placed for the enjoyment of the eighteenth-century visitor included a small building whose rather sinister name, 'The Rathouse', was reflected in its gothic windows and knobbly walls, and an atmospheric stone hermitage by the river. Today's visitor can easily be romanced by the beautiful poignancy of such

a feature, but would do well to remember that in the eighteenth century hermitages were often no more than fashionable garden commodities, usually providing an amusing attraction rather than fulfilling any more profound religious function. Ideally, the hermitage had an accompanying hermit, who might have been paid to play the part, rather like out-of-work actors are paid to play Santa in his grotto. These arrangements were often unsatisfactory however, because the hermits could rarely live up to the strict expectations that they would not talk, shave, or socialise. If a 'real' hermit could not be found, models were sometimes used. At least these were less likely to rebel against the strict rules!

In the eighteenth-century the Wilderness was a politer experience than its name suggested but in the twenty-first century Adlington's Wilderness is rapidly becoming genuinely wild. Maintenance has been short in this demanding area and so nature has broken its reins and has spectacularly wrested control of the landscape from man. Fallen trees have put down new roots and begin to grow afresh, with one fine specimen earning the name of 'Spider Tree'. Lush sprouting ferns nestle happily in the undergrowth and, in spring, a sea of bluebells glows in the dappled sunshine. Most of Charles Legh's sinuous paths have been lost to rogue rhododenrons and other undergrowth, although they are still visible in an Ordnance Survey map of 1909.[5] The once penetrable woodland has become dense due mainly to the undesirable addition of pines and sycamores and the buildings are rapidly being lost to the claws of nature.

The Tig House is still in good condition, although the tennis lawn is only fit for the games of the bunnies that bounce across it, but the Chinese Bridge lost its summerhouse many years ago. More recent is the virtual destruction of the Rathouse and of the Hermitage when weary trees fell on them. At the moment the Hermitage is being left as a pile of stones; it had been a virtual ruin during living memory anyway and the estate is reluctant to rebuild it without really knowing what it should look like. The remaining walls of the Rathouse are rapidly being obscured by a curtain of ivy, giving them a picturesque air that no doubt would have delighted Charles Legh, but unfortunately this is not doing the structure much good. In order to avoid such destruction, Father Tiber was moved many decades ago from his spot in the Wilderness to the much more civilized courtyard in front of the timbered east wing. The Temple of Diana still looks good, but closer inspection reveals that it is suffering from damp and could do with some tender loving care.

Head Gardener Steve Catchpole acknowledges all these things with a wry shake of his head but points out the immense cost of running such a property. In an estate of such size and complexity, every repair costs infinitely more than it does in a normal domestic home and, unfortunately, the grants that are normally available for heritage properties are less than forthcoming when the property concerned is owned by a private individual, the misguided perception being that the taxes of the 'average man' should not have to support the lifestyle

A collapsed 'Spider' tree lurks in the Wilderness.

of the wealthy. The cost of repairs to the Wilderness buildings has to be weighed against other demands: the Great Hall, which is of great architectural importance and brings in vital revenue as a wedding venue, recently needed to have its many-paned windows replaced, at a cost of £100,000. Mrs Camilla Legh, the current owner, was hoping that English Heritage would share the cost of the repairs, but was told that this would not be possible after its own finances suffered as a result of having to shut its properties during the foot and mouth outbreak of 2001.

Adlington is not entirely stuck in time however, waiting for decay to overtake it due to lack of funds. Cheaper garden projects which hold Mrs Legh's particular interest are going ahead, and so this garden is developing into a new stage of its life, a far cry from the National Trust properties, for example, where any changes are made in accordance to a strict historic management plan laboriously researched by professionals! So, the Wilderness Garden is currently undergoing something of

a revamp; Steve Catchpole, a man brimming over with friendly enthusiasm and energy, rallied his team, who number four at best, and cleared what had become an impenetrable hollow of rhododendrons and trees below Tiber's previous standpoint in order to create a new bog garden.

Nearer the house the taste of the current Legh to own Adlington has again asserted itself over that of Charles Legh in the eighteenth century. In the 1950s a garden was created for Father Tiber in the cobbled courtyard in front of the black and white wing of the house. This was unsatisfactory however and so, on coming to Adlington in 2000, one of Steve Catchpole's remits was to rebuild it. Accordingly, he has created a rectangular garden in which Tiber sits, tamed and domesticated, under a tree laden with pink blossom, watching over a

pretty scene complete with rectangular fish pool, rill and fountain. The backdrop to this garden is the high wall of the stable block, converted in the 1960s to desirable mews flats for renting, on which sit two unicorn heads that once mounted some gate pillars. In the courtyard itself, he has planted a new design inspired by knot gardens, although the tiny homegrown box plants are currently in a battle for survival against marauding rabbits.

Catchpole's other remit was to address the

Top & middle: Bluebells run riot in the Wilderness. Bottom: The Shell House sits on the edge of the Wilderness.

gardens to the north of the house. Charles Legh's water garden had turned to waste ground and when Mrs Legh came to Adlington some dozen years ago she had the area converted into a rose garden with a yew maze beyond. There were problems with drainage however and so the garden was not as successful as had been hoped. Catchpole tackled the problem however and designed and implemented an exuberant celebration of England's favourite flower, in which a pergola leads from the moat to a huge circular garden, framed by ropes draped with climbing roses. Unsurprisingly, it has been a resounding success with Adlington's visitors.

Yet although Mrs Legh may be able to decide what happens in her gardens, she does share them with Adlington's summer visitors, with the guests to the weddings and other events held there, and with the tenants of the mews flats in the stable block. The walled kitchen garden is therefore her refuge. Charmingly, Catchpole issued me with a blushing warning before pushing open the door to this corner of Adlington, which is not open to the public. In the twenty-first century as in the eighteenth, the walled garden is very much the working heart of the property. A funny hotchpotch, it today contains polytunnels and greenhouses so that the garden staff can save money by rearing the garden's shrubs and other plants 'in-house', a delightful cottage (rebuilt in the twentieth century following a fire) that is home to a well-known soap star, and a modern tennis court where Mrs Legh likes to entertain her friends in private. Hiding in one corner is Jupiter House, a brick cottage which was thought to have once formed part of the attractions of the Wilderness.[6]

So just as the Legh family enthusiastically left its mark on the Adlington landscape in the eighteenth century, it does so again in the twenty-first. As such, Catchpole enjoys the fact that the atmosphere at Adlington is a special one, which has attracted a close and motivated team of people to work there. Those with a passion for

The River Dene snakes through the Wilderness..

the gardens of the past will inevitably yearn to see its eighteenth-century landscape protected and brought back from the past but in the absence of this there is a certain pleasure in seeing a historic garden being used and enjoyed in the same personal way it was hundreds of years ago.

The Tig House is one of the many novelties to once grace Adlington.

Select Bibliography

de Figueiredo, Peter and Treuherz, Julian. *Cheshire County Houses*. Phillimore, Sussex, 1988.
English Heritage Register of Parks and Gardens of Special Historic Interest, 1999.
Harris, John. *The Artist and the Country House, from the Fifteenth Century to the Present Day*, Sotheby Pathe Bernet Publications, London, 1979.
Nares, Gordon. 'Adlington Hall, Cheshire - I'. *Country Life*, 28th November 1952, p1734-7.
Nares, Gordon, 'Adlington Hall, Cheshire - II'. *Country Life*, 12th December 1952, p1960-3.
Ordnance Survey 25" to 1 mile, Cheshire Sheet 28.8, 3rd edition 1909.
Ormerod, George. *The History of the County Palatine and City of Chester*. Volume 3, Lackington, Hughes, Harding, Mavor, and Jones, London, 1819.

References

1   *English Heritage Register of Parks and Gardens of Special Historic Interest*, 1999.
2   George Ormerod. *The History of the County Palatine and City of Chester*. Volume 3, 1819, p332.
3   Reproduced in John Harris. *The Artist and the Country House, from the Fifteenth Century to the Present Day*. 1979, p320.
4   *English Heritage Register of Parks and Gardens of Special Historic Interest*, 1999.
5   *Ordnance Survey 25" to 1 mile*, Cheshire Sheet 28.8, 3rd edition 1909.
6   *English Heritage Register of Parks and Gardens of Special Historic Interest*, 1999.

Lyme Park, Disley

A tract of land between the moors of Derbyshire and the rolling slopes of Cheshire, 240 metres above sea level, is not perhaps the site that first comes to a gardener's mind as the ideal location for his work. Nor is one that inspired a nineteenth-century writer to comment that the 'venerable Mansion … defies the wintry blast,' with the climate ensuring that any gardens are always a few weeks behind those only a few miles away.[1] This is however the location for Lyme Park, Disley, and, in fact, it is this striking landscape that makes Lyme so memorable.

Right from the outset, Lyme Park is filled with visual drama as today's visitor suddenly swings off the road from the affluent residential streets of Disley, through which he has approached, and, as if entering another world, finds himself in a commanding country estate which seems to demand absolute attention and respect. In 1855, Sir Bernard Burke wrote that: 'A broad and gently-winding highway, more than a mile in length, displays the peculiar features of the Park, which is extensive, and like all around it exceedingly wild and romantic.'[2] Lyme Park has been preserved so well that Burke could just as easily have been describing it in the early twenty-first century as in the nineteenth, although the exact line of the drive has varied slightly over the years, now running below those of Burke's day and earlier. The drive up to the house is long and undulating, weaving through the hilly park, and so serves to build a feeling of suspense, heightened by a mysterious square tower that watches our progress from its perch above the approach. Then our courage is rewarded when, suddenly, the house in all its classical splendour appears in view, sitting firmly and proudly in a dip, behind the austere protective gates of a railed forecourt.

By passing through the house, which is built around an internal courtyard, the visitor can enter the gardens, which are manicured and gracious. Yet as he strolls on the polite lawns, his view is distracted by glimpses of the surrounding park where intriguingly enigmatic structures loom. It is not long before he is tempted out into the park which slopes up on all sides

Above: A short walk leads from the Hall at Lyme to the Cage beyond.

The view from Paddock Cottage is magnificent.

Paddock Cottage sits high in Lyme Park.

A charming fountain plays in the Orangery.

The replanted flower borders burst with life.

from the garden, and comes to appreciate the stunning setting of Lyme Park with the wild open moorland of Derbyshire seeming desperate to swoop in and encroach on the civilisation of the designed landscape.

Originally part of the Macclesfield hunting 'forest', Lyme's park was enclosed in the fourteenth century by its first owner, Piers Legh I, and in the seventeenth century began to become ornamental when his descendant Richard Legh created avenues of sycamore and lime in a goose foot effect. One such avenue was planted with limes to lead the eye from the house up to the southern tip of the park, and this still exists today. Following extensive storm damage in 1980, it was replanted during Lyme's management by the local town council, but unfortunately a slapdash approach meant that the 'wrong' type of lime was used, creating a bushy rather than linear effect. This has since been corrected by the National Trust who introduced trees which had been specially nurtured in their nursery at Dunham Massey

and which were actually descendants of Richard Legh's trees.

Richard Legh's avenues were kept by his son Peter XII when he undertook a programme of extensive tree planting in the park, developing it largely into the form that exists today. The park's most distinctive feature is the buildings scattered through it, and Peter XII ensured that there were sight lines to each of these through the trees as they acted as embellishments to the natural landscape. The stone tower glimpsed on the approach to the house is the Cage, and as it can be reached by a pleasant stroll from the car park, it is probably the most visited of Lyme's features. Perched on the brow of a hill to the north of the house, the Cage commands a spectacular view of the surrounding countryside, and is itself immensely picturesque with blocky turrets and many staring windows. A tower has been on this site since the sixteenth century and it is thought that the Cage earned its evocative name by acting as a prison for poachers,[3] but it would

Lyme is instantly recognisable across the south lawn

have been used primarily as a banqueting or hunting lodge. The current structure is believed to have been designed by the prominent eighteenth- century Italian architect Giacomo Leoni, who is responsible for much of the current house, giving it the Palladian look it has today.[4] Visitors who walk the distance from the house are rewarded by being able to climb the spiral staircase in one of the turrets. Entering from the basement space, we ascend to a first-floor room that was restored by architect Lewis Wyatt in the nineteenth century, and the service room at the top, from which the views are fantastic.

Also well worth the steep walk is the gaunt-looking Paddock Cottage, which was erected as a functional building by Peter IX, even before Richard Legh began his work on the park. This recently restored building perches defiantly on the edge of the park looking over the moorland to one side and Cheshire fields to the other, making it a charming spot to have a picnic, although unfortunately the Cottage itself is only open occasionally. Further east of here are the remains of a Stag House, once featuring at the end of the lime avenue but now sadly in ruins.

An eighteenth-century turret-shaped building known as the Lantern hangs to the east of the house, seemingly suspended from the hillside. According to Gary Raynsford, Lyme's current head gardener, the tradition was that as long as you could see the Lantern from the garden, it was a good day to go hunting. Indeed, in the twentieth century a chunk was cut from a yew on the east terrace to ensure a direct line of sight to the Lantern from the dining table. It is no wonder that the residents of Lyme have exhibited such an eagerness for hunting, as it was home to a breed of red deer that had the privilege of having been hunted by James, Duke of York, during a 1676 visit.[5] An unusual breed of large white wild cattle also made Lyme their home, probably merely continuing an occupancy that had been established before the park was enclosed, but these eventually became extinct at the end of the nineteenth century. Not

everyone shared the attachment to Lyme of the wild cattle however. Victorian visitor W Adam sniffed that: 'the park, which is stocked with red deer, is more like an uncultivated waste'.[6]

Whilst the park at Lyme is aloof and haunting, the garden surrounding the house is insistently refined and splendid, having evolved over many generations of the Legh family. A seventeenth-century painting shows a walled forecourt to the north of the house, and tree-filled areas directly to the west, a grass parterre and fountain to the side of the forecourt, and terraces to the east.[7] A century later, an engraving by W Watts, from a drawing by Claude Nates, reveals a cascade thought to have been constructed around 1700, which flows down from the pond in the south lawn to a millpond further west. It shows a pond in the south lawn on which people fish from a small boat, with a gate in the walled balustrade to the west, presumably through which the water was allowed to flow and create the cascade effect.[8] The cascade was eventually abolished by Lewis Wyatt in the early nineteenth-century, but the pond on the south lawn still exists. So too does the millpond, although it is now bordered by a car park and early twentieth-century Arts and Crafts style buildings that were originally used to house the estate's workshops, laundry, and electricity plant, before becoming the National Trust tearoom.

Lewis Wyatt's removal of the cascade and restoration of the Cage was part of a scheme of works he carried out at Lyme for Thomas Legh in the early nineteenth century, mainly orientated around the house.[9] He introduced the natural contours of the pond on the south lawn, and in doing so created what has become one of the most famous garden views of our age.[10] There cannot be many visitors to Lyme who do not gasp at the stunning sight of the south front from across the pond, and recognise it as Elizabeth's first view of Pemberley in the television adaptation of Jane Austen's *Pride and Prejudice*. Even more famously, the south pond at Lyme currently enjoys the claim to fame of being the water through which Elizabeth, and a nation of twentieth-century female fans, enjoyed watching Mr Darcy wade in a controversial scene that appeared in the recent television programme but not in the novel. This celebrity may be one of Lyme Park's least 'serious' claims to fame, but it has had very real benefits: Gary Raynsford claims that overnight it catapulted the property's visitor numbers to the level that it had previously expected to take six years to reach. On the far side of the lake is a gentle ravine decorated with naturalistic plantings such as primulas, hostas and ferns. At the top of this is a stone bridge, and at the bottom the water flows through a culvert to the lake. This area is called Killtime, and legend has it that this is because it was a favourite hang-out for gardeners wanting, quite literally, to kill time.

One of Lyme's most famous features is the Dutch Garden that rests sunken behind the buttress to the west below the south lawn, where once the cascade flowed, and this was created by the 1st Lord Newton, Thomas Legh's nephew who succeeded in 1857, and was made a peer in 1892.[11] The visitor is drawn to the terraced walk that edges the lawn by the promise of a view that any raised area offers. Then his eye is drawn down to a small square garden at the foot of the deep buttress and held by a distinctive ivy-edged parterre, with bright planting and central feature of a fountain representing the four elements, Earth, Air, Fire and Water. In creating this garden, Lord Newton is said to have been advised by designer Edward Kemp. Kemp's book *How to Lay Out a Small Garden* expounds the benefits of tucking away areas such as this one, which are of a different style to the rest of the garden, so that the overall view is still harmonious: 'What is meant is, that a garden, as viewed from the house, or from most of its own principal points, should consist of parts and objects that have some decided agreement with each other, or that the several constituent parts should blend and interfuse insensibly; while peculiarities, whether of treatment of vegetation, can be reserved for little side scenes, shut off from the rest, or most imperfectly disclosed, until the

observer finds himself all at once in the midst of them. The full effect of a contrast may thus be secured, without any interference with the much more important principles of harmony or congruity.'[12] This area had to have a new drainage system installed by the National Trust because the previous one had deteriorated so that the area was wet and cold, causing the ivy-edging to die away. Gary Raynsford explains that to provide a spectacular display, this area is currently planted with a stunning 15,000 spring bulbs, and then the same again in summer. He believes however that when the parterre was designed, it would have only have been planted for the summer, as the family would not have been resident in the spring. Such a system would prove disappointing to the typical National Trust visitor however, who can turn up at any time between March and the end of October and expect a show. The nineteenth-century planting would most probably have been based instead on semi-permanent summer bedding and this rather more labour-friendly approach is one that Gary hopes to return to, not least because he now runs his gardens with four staff, one apprentice, and some dedicated volunteers, compared to the fifteen gardeners of the 'old days'. We always marvel at the number of gardeners it took to maintain a garden before the advent of better tools and machinery, but in fact they must have not worked quite round the clock, as the origins of the name 'Killtime' testify!

We also have to thank the 1st Lord Newton for the completion of the Orangery which had been begun by Wyatt to the east of the house. Having suffered for several decades when it was used as a tearoom, this is now resplendent once more with a charming modern fountain playing, and a pair of tree ferns planted recently to welcome the visitor at the doorway. These newcomers are monitored from the back wall by a century-old fig and two huge but unidentified pinky-red camellias, which are thought to date from around the same time as the Orangery was built.

The Orangery opens out onto a terrace, which in turn descends with a small flight of steps through its rough buttress to the South Lawn. This East Terrace is set out with a green lawn divided by wide gravel paths and punctuated by formal flowerbeds which, like the Dutch Garden, have two planting schemes each year, using the *Penstemon* 'Rubicunda' which was raised specifically for Lyme in 1906. Nearest the house are a pair of sundial-shaped beds, then are two sunken crossbeds, at the centre is a magnificent bed in the shape of a wheel with eight spokes, and last, providing a fine sight in front of the Orangery doorway are a further two crossbeds, this time not sunken. A writer in *Country Life* of 1904 was very complimen-

The East Terrace is a fine sight with its sundial beds & sunken crossbeds.

tary about this garden as he saw it: 'Fine urns, vases, statues, and an excellent marble sundial are features not to be overlooked.'[13]

During the occupancy of the 2nd Lord Newton, who succeeded in 1898, the slope to the west of the house was planted with many shrubs from a family friend, the plantsman Vicary Gibbs, including a variegated sycamore (*Acer pseudoplatanus* 'Leopoldii') and a Chinese Cornel (*Cornus kousa*). His wife Lady Evelyn also created the rose garden next to the Orangery, on the site of two sunken pit greenhouses. This corner benefited from the National Trust centenary in 1995 with a celebratory restoration, although it exploits the benefits of modern varieties of roses rather than remaining slavishly loyal to those chosen by Lady Newton in 1913. Today its simple grey paving is punctuated by roses, mainly pink, with a delightful scent, making this a pleasantly feminine corner of these otherwise showy gardens. Lady Newton was passionate about Lyme Park, writing *The House of Lyme*, and *Lyme Letters*, detailed histories of Lyme and its occupants. In *Lyme Letters* her love of the place shines through: 'And here I may mention that nowhere in any part of Europe or the East that I have visited – and I have travelled a good deal – have I seen anything to compare to the autumn sunsets at Lyme. Whether from the atmosphere, or from what other cause I know not, but the gorgeous colouring of the sunset sky, lit up with every variety of pink, red, crimson and orange, shading into deepest purple, made a picture few artists could do full justice to.'[14]

The 3rd Lord Newton's wife, Lady Helen, created narrow flower borders to the east of the rose garden, but these were replanted in the 1960s by Graham Stuart Thomas, Gardens Advisor to the National Trust. Now these are wide borders with two in 'hot' colours such as red, orange and yellow, and two in 'cool' colours such as pinks, purple and white. In his book on the gardens of the National Trust, Stuart Thomas explained the reasons behind this replanting: 'With less staff to manage them the trim herbaceous borders have been replanted mostly with plants that do not require staking, following a colour scheme from end to end.'[15] Stuart Thomas was also responsible for the planting scheme of the impressive borders below the East Terrace. Against the rough stone wall these burst with colour contrasting well with the calm green of the South Lawn. Raynsford has preserved the plantings as Stuart Thomas intended them in the belief that, with time, Stuart Thomas, who died in Spring 2003, will be an iconic garden figure.

Having passed in front of the Orangery, the visitor finds himself looking down once more, this time to a small railed garden at the eastern side of the forecourt. This garden was originally planted by Lewis Wyatt in 1812 and was restored in 2001, having suffered as a tennis court and car park, and now uses authentic plantings to make it a rare example of Wyatt's garden design. It was in fact thanks to *Pride and Prejudice* that this work was carried out as it was funded by the widower of a great fan, who wished the garden to testify as a memorial to his wife.

Lyme Park's status as one of the jewels in the National Trust crown is thanks to its having been bequeathed to the Trust in 1946 by the 3rd Lord Newton, Richard. Leasing Lyme from the National Trust, the Stockport Corporation (town council) then ran the estate for several decades with varying degrees of success, until in 1994 the Trust took over direct management using an annual financial contribution from the Corporation. This lofty mansion with its ruggedly handsome park and gracious gardens has perhaps been rather humbled by having to endure the hundreds of thousands of visitors who now swarm over it. In this remote setting they play frisbee in the park, coo over the colours on the East Lawn, and dream of fictional heros wading through the South Pond. This though reflects today's more egalitarian society, just as Lyme Park in its earlier days reflected the elite lifestyle of the British aristocracy. Thus it has happily managed to remain useful and relevant well after the family that created it has moved on.

Select Bibliography

Adam, W. *The Gem of the Peak*. 1851.
Burke, Sir Bernard. *A Visitation of the Seats and Arms of the Noblemen and Gentlemen of Great Britain*. Series 2, Volume 1, Hurst and Blackett, London, 1855.
Cornforth, John. 'Lyme Park, Cheshire - I'. *Country Life*, 5th December 1974, p1724-27.
'Lyme Hall, Cheshire: The Seat of Lord Newton'. *Country Life*, 17th December 1904, p906-915.
English Heritage Register of Parks and Gardens of Special Historic Interest, 1999.
Kemp, Edward. *How to Lay Out a Small Garden*. Bradbury and Evans, London, 1850.
Neale, JP. *Views of the Seats of Noblemen and Gentlemen, in England, Wales, Scotland, and Ireland*. Second Series, Volume 1, Sherwood, Jones and co., 1824.
Newton, Lady. *Lyme Letters 1660-1760*. William Heinemann, London, 1925.
Ormerod, George, *The History of the County Palatine and City of Chester*. Volume 3, Lackington, Hughes, Harding, Mavor, and Jones, London, 1819.
Rothwell, James. *Lyme Park*. National Trust Enterprises, London, 1998.
Stuart Thomas, Graham. *Gardens of the National Trust*. Book Club Associates, London, 1979.
Watts, W. *The Seats of the Nobility and Gentry In a Collection of the Most Interesting and Picturesque Views*. W. Watts, Chelsea, 1779.

References

1   JP Neale. *Views of the Seats of Noblemen and Gentlemen, in England, Wales, Scotland, and Ireland*. Second Series, Volume 1, 1824.
2   Sir Bernard Burke. *A Visitation of the Seats and Arms of the Noblemen and Gentlemen of Great Britain*. Series 2, Volume 1, 1855, p35.
3   Lady Newton. *Lyme Letters 1660-1760*. 1925, p102.
4   'Lyme Hall, Cheshire: The Seat of Lord Newton'. *Country Life*, 17th December 1904, p914.
5   James Rothwell. *Lyme Park*. 1998, p44.
6   W Adam. *The Gem of the Peak*. 1851, p325.
7   Reproduced in James Rothwell. *Lyme Park*. 1998, p41.
8   W Watts. *The Seats of the Nobility and Gentry In a Collection of the Most Interesting & Picturesque Views*. 1779, Plate LXXIX.
9   'Lyme Hall, Cheshire: The Seat of Lord Newton'. *Country Life*, 17th December 1904, p914.
10 James Rothwell. *Lyme Park*, 1998, p40.
11 'Lyme Hall, Cheshire: The Seat of Lord Newton'. *Country Life*, 17th December 1904, p912.
12 Edward Kemp. *How to Lay Out a Small Garden*. 1850, p72.
13 'Lyme Hall, Cheshire: The Seat of Lord Newton'. *Country Life*, 17th December 1904, p915.
14 Lady Newton. *Lyme Letters 1660-1760*. 1925, p3.
15 Graham Stuart Thomas. *Gardens of the National Trust*. 1979, p167.

Top: A small Lewis Wyatt garden sits below the East Terrace

Tatton Park, Knutsford

*T*atton Park is today one of Cheshire's favourite visitor attractions, having come under the joint control of the National Trust and Cheshire County Council after the last Lord Egerton, Maurice, died in 1958. It woos crowds with a fabulous combination of house, park and gardens, in which famous names such as Samuel and Lewis Wyatt, Humphry Repton and Joseph Paxton have all played a part, offering, to borrow an over-used tourist brochure phrase, 'something for everyone'.

The Egertons had owned the Old Hall at Tatton since it was bought from the Brereton family in 1598 by Sir Thomas Egerton, but by the end of the seventeenth century it had become home to John Egerton who felt that something a little more substantial was required. In 1716 he completed a new house on the site of today's mansion but as the family continued to go from strength to strength, even this building became inadequate. Between 1780 and 1813 the architect Samuel Wyatt and then his nephew Lewis each took their turn to remodel the house until it achieved the neo-classical style we see today.

As with so many grand properties, just as the house evolved, so has the landscape surrounding it. At Tatton however the real marvel is that the alterations did not usually replace previous designs, but rather were added on to the early gardens, simply eating up more and more park. This means that the different periods of garden history witnessed at Tatton are not so much layers one on top of each other, but rather sit side by side so that the visitor can walk through time from one to another.

The early eighteenth-century house would have had parkland virtually right up to the door, although there was some element of

58

Top: Tatton Park's Japanese Garden has been beautifully restored.
Inset: Statue from the Lady Anna's rose garden.

The Japanese Garden is a serene place.

*A simple wooden door leads to
the Tower Garden.*

*A terrace stretches the Hall
and the Italian garden.*

Below: The Italian Garden sits below the Hall.

garden: to the north was a formal semi-circular pond, to the east and west were formal lines of trees (these could have been either orchard or yew walk), and the south front was occupied by a walled garden, probably used to supply the kitchen.[1] There was a tree-framed vista to the north that became known as Lady Mary's Walk, still existing today, and on succeeding in 1738, Samuel Egerton set out a beech avenue vista to the south, despite having financial difficulties that forced him to let Tatton.[2] This is today the Broad Walk through the gardens, having become an ornamental feature when a new drive to the house was created.

Fortunately, an inheritance meant that the Egertons returned to better financial fortune, and they used some of this money to improve Tatton, bringing first William Emes and then renowned landscape architect Humphry Repton to revise the park. Repton had strong views on the approach to houses and so designed a new drive through grand entrance gates at the Knutsford end, curving round to the east before reaching the house. As he explains in his description of Tatton in *Sketches and Hints on Landscape Gardening*, its impact is due to a large degree on its size, but Repton resolved to lead the visitor to the house via a circuitous drive that passed all the most impressive parts of the park: 'It is not from the situation only that the character of Tatton derives its greatness. The command of the adjoining property, the style and magnitude of the mansion, and all its appendages, contribute to confer that degree of importance which ought here to be the leading object in every plan of improvement.

'Vastness of extent will no more constitute greatness of character in a park, than a vast pile of differently coloured buildings will constitute greatness of character in a house. A park, from its vast extent, may perhaps surprise, but it will not impress us with the character of greatness and importance, unless we are led to those parts where beauty is shewn to exist, with all its interest, amidst the boundless range of undivided property.'[3] The drive which Repton designed to fulfil this function still exists today and is that which leads from Knutsford and past the meres to the house.

One of the main reasons for Repton's fame having endured through the centuries is his pro-

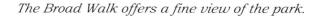

The Broad Walk offers a fine view of the park.

lific use of the pen. He compiled his proposals into a Red Book for each property, so called because they were quite literally books with red covers, in which the chief gimmick was to use careful paper flaps to illustrate a 'before and after' view of the landscape on which he would be working his magic. This must have enthralled his clients and today acts as an invaluable research tool as well as captivating even the most world-weary garden historian! At Tatton, such flaps were employed by Repton to demonstrate his ideas of how to solve the problem of that distinctly Cheshire landscape feature, the mere.

People from outside of Cheshire are often nonplussed by the concept of a mere, as opposed to a lake, and Repton offers an explanation which is as good as any: 'It has often been asserted by authors on gardening, that all pieces of fresh water must come under one of these descriptions, – a lake, a pool, a river, or a rivulet: but since my acquaintance with Cheshire, I am inclined to add the meer, as an intermediate term between the lake and the pool; it being, frequently, too large to be deemed a pool, and too small, as well as too round in its form, to deserve the name of a lake: for the beauty of a lake consists not so much in its size, as in those deep bays and bold promontories which prevent the eye from ranging over its whole surface.'[4] Tatton today has two meres, Tatton Mere and Melchett Mere, the latter now being the largest of the two, having begun to appear in the 1920s as the result of subsidence following brine extraction. When Repton visited, Melchett Mere was of course yet to form but there were nevertheless two meres because to the north of Tatton Mere, just below the house, was Turn Mere, where there is now the White Walk and Turn Mere Glade. Repton was a great fan of stretches of naturalistic water in a view, but he felt strongly that two smaller patches just did not create the right effect compared to one large expanse.

61

Top & bottom: A before (top) & after (bottom) of Repton's proposed works to the meres at Tatton, from his Red Book. (Tatton Park - Cheshire County Council).

Thus he expended a great deal of energy writing about, and illustrating with flaps, the advantage of manipulating the meres at Tatton to create the effect of their being one: 'What is best respecting these two large meers in Tatton Park, is a question of some difficulty, and on which there has been a variety of opinions. I shall now proceed to deliver mine, and endeavour to explain the reasons on which it is founded.

'An unity of design in all compositions is, confessedly, one of the first principles in each of the polite arts; and nothing, perhaps, evinces more strongly the love of unity acting on the mind in landscape gardening, than the following fact, viz. that the most superficial observer of any park scene will be displeased by the view of two separate pieces of water; and he will probably ask, without reflecting on the differences of levels, why they are not formed into one? The first opinion seems, therefore, that these two waters should be united: but if the union is not clearly possible, it certainly ought not to be attempted. The second opinion, is that the upper pool ought to be destroyed; or, as some express themselves, should be filled up: but the latter would be an Herculean labour to very little purpose; and the former, though practicable, would not be advisable, because so deep an hollow immediately in front of the house, would be a yawning chasm, very difficult to convert into an object of beauty. My opinion, therefore is, that the two waters should from the house, appear to be connected with each other, although in reality they are very far asunder ... The large piece of water

crosses the eye in the view from the house; consequently it looks much less considerable than it really is, and its effect is of little advantage to the scene, being too distant, and too widely separated by the vast tract of low ground betwixt the pool and the lake. I propose that this water should be rendered more interesting, by making it appear as if the arm of a river proceeded from the lake; and its termination will be easily hid in the valley.'[5]

Repton's advice was not taken immediately, but historian George Ormerod records that the landscape architect John Webb was employed in 1816 to drain Turn Mere 'on account of its proximity to the house'.[6] Indeed, Repton's insistence that it would be difficult to fill the space left by the mere is proven wrong by the pleasantness of a stroll through the wooded garden, known as White Walk, which now takes its place. In spite of this however, Repton's desire for only one patch of water was again refused with the appearance of Melchett Mere. Yet, in a further twist of fate, Melchett Mere is gradually and mysteriously expanding and, if it continues, will eventually join with Tatton Mere so that Repton may still get his much-desired united mere!

With the park taking shape, the gardens began to slowly accumulate. In 1814 Lewis Wyatt created what became known as 'Charlotte's Garden', the charming and refined area that today greets the visitor when they emerge through the walled garden entrance. In his simple but effective design the lawn is engraved with curving paths and scattered with magnolias, hollies and small pines. The original de-

Top: Charlotte's Garden is a charming & refined area.
Bottom: Tatton's mysterious tower watches over the gardens.

Above: Splendid topiary surrounds the rose garden.
Below: The Italian Garden is best admired from above.

sign shows plantings of roses, dahlias, ericas, daphnes, rhododendrons and azaleas.[7] The focus of this area is a mounded star-shaped flowerbed with bold bedding plants, and the scene is watched by Lady Charlotte's Arbour, a delightful treillage seat. In 1847, a fountain was added to the scene and these component features – curved paths, lawn, flowerbed, arbour, fountain – make this garden typical of the period, when an obviously artificial style of design was being celebrated after so many years of the landscape park.

Wyatt also built a gracious sandstone conservatory, or orangery, which was joined to the house via a glass passageway, although this integral link was lost in the 1930s when Maurice de Tatton Egerton built the Tenants Hall in its place. The conservatory still exists and the plants grown in here provide a lush tropical feel with palms, citrus plants, and climbers such as the passion flower. It is a very English experience to be able to stand in the steamy jungle of the conservatory and look through its glass

walls to the lawn outside.

The 1830s saw the arrival of a copy of the Choragic Monument of Lysicrates in Athens, which was placed as a focus at the end of the Broad Walk, being a great incentive to walk the length of the avenue. This was a commemoration of Wilbraham Egerton's Grand Tour, a ritual undertaken by wealthy young gentlemen in this period (rather like today's young students take 'Gap Years' to travel before university), without which the great English gardens we enjoy today would be much duller places, lacking the inspiration of these foreign visits. All along the Broad Walk are natural garden areas including the Leech Pool, whose horrible name belies its beauty, especially in the autumn when the huge Royal Ferns (Osmunda regalis) surrounding this sheltered pool turn a brilliant bronze colour. More attractively named is the Golden Brook, which has been considered part of the garden for centuries but was previously a brick clay pit. It is now one of the quieter, less visited parts of Tatton, with gentle grass banks surrounding a sinuous pool which looks as though it could have been there forever.

In 1847, the terrace on the south front of the house was laid-out by Edward Milner as an 'Italian Garden' to a design by Joseph Paxton.[8] Paxton spent much of his life as Head Gardener at Chatsworth, property of the Devonshires in Derbyshire, and became hugely influential in Victorian garden design. By the time he created the Tatton Italian Garden, he had already designed Birkenhead Park, Merseyside, and was soon to design the Crystal Palace at the 1851 Great Exhibition for Prince Albert. This terrace at Tatton, which overlooks the park and meres, is today one of the most famous scenes in Cheshire, with ornate flower-filled parterres centred on huge urns and a small quatrefoil pool with a statue of Triton. In fact, this statue and also the Ruabon stone balustrade around the garden was added by The 2nd Baron Egerton in 1883.

The Victorian age was a great one for trends: rockeries, orchids and carpet bedding all enjoyed their turn. One such craze was for ferns, which could be planted in both rockeries or in glasshouses, and this was a fashion to which the Egertons clearly succumbed. Tatton's celebrated fernery to the west of the conservatory was built in 1859 by Joseph Paxton's assistant and son-in-law George Stokes, so perhaps Paxton had a hand here too. The fernery is tucked away, appearing almost to be part of the garden walls, and today the visitor enters through a unassuming domestic door which would seem to lead to an unremarkable greenhouse, but actually grants access to a narrow twisting path through what feels like a ravine, wallpapered with the Creeping Fig (*Ficus pumila*) and planted densely with *Dicksonia* tree ferns. These were brought from New Zealand and by the end of the nineteenth century had grown so tall that the roof had to be raised to its present height.[9] Fortunately the roof should not need to be raised again as the ferns can in fact be cut down and started afresh.

If Paxton brought a flavour of Italy to Tatton,

albeit in a form probably not recognisable to the Italians, then Japan arrived here in the early years of the twentieth century. Just as Victorian Tatton embraced the fashion for ferneries, Edwardian Tatton embraced the current fashion for Japanese Gardens. Generally speaking, such gardens, which sprung up at all kinds of properties in Great Britain, were genuinely inspired by the gardens of Japan, but took on their own form, making them almost unrecognisable to a Japanese visitor. In 1910 Alan de Tatton, the 3rd Baron Egerton, created a Japanese tea garden that was more authentic than most, perhaps thanks to the help of his team of Kyoto workmen. The mossy ground in this area is undulating and filled with twisting streams and paths. Views of the garden offer peaceful scenes of a thatched tea-house on an island, a Shinto Temple, curved bridge, and other Japanese garden features. All are framed with mosses, conifers and maples, whose foliage turn brilliantly fiery in the autumn. This is

Opposite page: The Conservatory is full of exotic plants.
Below: A charming pavilion overlooks the rose garden.

not a garden for wandering through it looks so delicate as to be trampled to death by Tatton's hoards of visitors. Rather it is allowed to rest serenely whilst we can view it from across a little wooden fence.

A few years after the success with the Japanese garden, a more English style (albeit with an Italian touch) was represented when a rose garden was laid out for Alan's wife, Lady Anna.

This walled corner has a private feel to it and its sunken form, based around a fountain, encourages one to sit and admire the scene, perhaps in the open-fronted pavilion, through the back window of which the kitchen garden can also be viewed. The roses lead into another secluded compartment, the Tower Garden. The square brick tower is rather an enigma, but is thought to have stood on this spot for many centuries, when it possibly acted as a park feature, either as an eyecatcher or to imprison poachers, rather like at Lyme.[10] Its drama is exaggerated because in such a small enclosed garden it is impossible to stand back and get a distanced view. Rather than the intimacy of its location causing the tower to be humbled, it forces us to crane our necks to see it looming large. A romantic wooden door leads from the Tower Garden out into the very mature Arboretum, which contains many impressive trees including pines, acers and sorbus.

After the 3rd Baron's introductions, one other foreign feature was added: the African Hut brought by Maurice Egerton, the last Egerton to own Tatton, to remind him of the faraway continent he so enjoyed but was unable to visit amidst the turmoil of the Second World War. This still stands next to the Broad Walk, where it squats looking very content, if slightly out-of-place.

So Tatton contains elements from many centuries, but since the arrival of the National Trust it has been rather frozen in time, although well-preserved. Sam Youd, Tatton's robustly confident Head Gardener of over twenty years, is adamant that he will eventually get his own way and be allowed to dedicate a new corner, beyond the Japanese Garden, to garden design of the twentieth, and eventually twenty-first century. Getting permission for such a bold idea is likely to be an uphill struggle but in the meantime Youd has made good use of his energies, satisfying himself with successful restoration projects.

In 2001, fuelled by his longstanding passion for China and Japan and helped by Professor Fukuhara from the Osaka University of Art, Youd completed a restoration of the Japanese

Opposite: The Arboretum provides a pleasant walk in any season.
Below: The Japanese Garden bursts with dramatic colour.

Garden, which had become overgrown and scruffy with water features, steps, paths and rustic bridge being lost. Oversized plantings were even more of a problem in this garden than in most, because the key to Japanese landscape design is the 'borrowed view' in which the scene beyond the boundaries of the garden is included in the design to make the site seem more blessed with size and features than it really is. Obviously then, if the planting has grown so large that the exterior view can no

longer be seen and 'borrowed', the garden has lost a vital feature.

The most recent restoration at Tatton is the ongoing project to return the kitchen gardens to glory, with work including the reconstruction of the fighouses, vineries, and pot plant house. In the twentieth century these gardens had become barren and disused but their importance should not be overlooked. When opinionated and opinion-forming garden writer John Claudius Loudon wrote his

Encyclopedia of Gardening in 1822, Tatton was one of the handful of Cheshire gardens that he considered worthy of comment, in this case because: 'the kitchen garden is large, and contains a spacious well-constructed pinery, and shady border for mosses'.[11] The restoration work includes a return of appropriate planting, with a fruit garden, vegetable garden and cut-flower borders. Many of the stock of these gardens originally came from the local nursery firm, Caldwells. This firm endured for centuries as a family business based in Knutsford and supplied many of the great houses nearby, such as Peover, Dunham Massey, Arley, Brereton, Capesthorne and Tabley. Both Tatton and Peover still used it for plant supplies until re-cently when it closed down amidst a row involving planning consent for the larger premises it sought. Fortunately, many of its catalogues and order books survive in the Cheshire Record Office and tell us, for example, that eighteenth-century Tatton was supplied with many things including '13 Green Curld Brocoly'[12] and dwarf Morello Cherry trees,[13] as well as flowers including double Dutch Hyacinth and white crocus.[14] It is a shame that Caldwells has not survived to supply the kitchen garden once more – that would have brought the project a wonderful authenticity that money and research alone cannot provide, but at least the gardens it helped to create are being given a new lease of life.

There are plenty of interesting features in the Japanese Garden.

Select Bibliography

Allen, David Elliston. *The Victorian Fern Craze: A History of Pteridomania*. Hutchinson, London, 1969.

English Heritage Register of Parks and Gardens of Special Historic Interest, 1999.

Loudon, JC. *Encyclopedia of Gardening*. London, 1822.

Ormerod, George. *The History of the County Palatine and City of Chester*. Volume 1, Lackington, Hughes, Harding, Mavor, and Jones, London, 1819.

Oswald, Arthur. 'Tatton Park Cheshire - III'. *Country Life*, 30th July 1964, p292-6.

Preliminary Historic Landscape Appraisal, Draft, Volume 1, Parklands Consortium, 2002.

Repton, Humphry. *Sketches and Hints on Landscape Gardening*. W. Bulmer & Co, London, 1794.

Roper, Lanning. 'A Garden on a Grand Scale'. *Country Life*, 8th April 1976, p884-886.

Youd, Sam, and McKean, Maggie. *Tatton Park: The Gardens*. Cheshire County Council, Cheshire, 1998.

'Tatton Park, Cheshire: The Seat of Earl Egerton of Tatton'. *Country Life*, 24th March 1906, p414-21.

The archive material used for Caldwells is held in the Cheshire Record Office.

References

1   *Preliminary Historic Landscape Appraisal*, Draft, Volume 1, 2002, p11.
2   *Preliminary Historic Landscape Appraisal*, Draft, Volume 1, 2002, p11.
3   Humphry, Repton. *Sketches and Hints on Landscape Gardening*. 1794, p9.
4   Humphry, Repton. *Sketches and Hints on Landscape Gardening*. 1794, p30.
5   Humphry, Repton. *Sketches and Hints on Landscape Gardening*. 1794, p31.
6   George Ormerod. *The History of the County Palatine and City of Chester*. Volume 1, 1819, p347.
7   *Preliminary Historic Landscape Appraisal*, Draft, Volume 1, 2002, p24.
8   *English Heritage Register of Parks and Gardens of Special Historic Interest*, 1999.
9   Sam Youd and Maggie McKean. *Tatton Park: The Gardens*. 1998, p33.
10 *Preliminary Historic Landscape Appraisal*, Draft, Volume 1, 2002, p19.
11 JC, Loudon. *Encyclopedia of Gardening*. 1822, p1244.
12 Cheshire Record Office DDX 363/6, 1789.
13 Cheshire Record Office DDX 363/6, 1790 and 1791.
14 Cheshire Record Office DDX 363/6, 1789.

Eatôn Hall, Chester

*T*here cannot be a garden lover in the country who has not created a fantasy garden based on the premise of money not being an issue. To convey the excitement of Eaton Hall then, I probably need say little more than it is that very daydream come true. It is the home of the 6th Duke and Duchess of Westminster, owners of a large chunk of London, including Belgravia and Mayfair, and as such is receiving every attention that money can buy. And it shows!

The land south of Chester came into the possession of the Grosvenor family in the fifteenth-century, and a house was first built there in the seventeenth century by Sir Thomas Grosvenor. In the early nineteenth century the house was rebuilt on a grand scale by his descendant, the first Grosvenor to be given the title of Marquess of Westminster in 1831.[1] This house was then remodelled by the second Marquess, and again by the third, who was made Duke of Westminster in 1874. In 1901, *Country Life* said that Eaton had had a 'somewhat singular architectural history',[2] but this was only to get worse as during the Second World War the house was occupied by the army, who treated it so badly that it eventually had to be demolished. The main house on the estate was thus for several years no more than a simple wooden building, until the 1970s when John Dennys, the 5th Duke's brother-in-law, designed what turned out apparently to be a rather unsatisfactorily modern house looking something like an office block. In the 1990s this was reduced to a shell, and extensive work carried out to give it a pinky casing, an extra floor and a boxy grey roof, creating the appearance of a French château. All this building work leads to great interest for the garden lover as the gardens were repeatedly reborn to keep up with the architecture.

The latest rebirth is currently an ongoing process, having begun in the early 1990s when the 6th Duke and Duchess decided to make the transition from using Eaton as a stopover in their busy lives, to investing the effort needed to make it a real home. In previous decades the gardens had held little of their attention and so had inevitably become neglected with, at one point, only two

Top: Designer Arabella Lennox-Boyd has recently replanted the herb garden. Inset: Stone Talbot dog in the herb garden.

The kitchen garden is organic wherever possible, and makes the most of complementry planting using wildflowers to control the insects.

The Italian Garden is planted in hazy shades.

A bold design gives the Italian Garden instant impact.

Below: Arabella Lennox-Boyd's pink garden compartment.

garden staff to take care of them, as opposed to the fifty-nine reportedly employed in the 1920s.

One of these two gardeners was Les Armstrong, who is now Head Gardener in charge of a much happier team of ten, and who is rejoicing in the garden's renaissance after his twenty-nine years of service. Armstrong has obviously been intensely involved in all the changes to the gardens, which he cites as one of the main reasons why he feels such a deep love for them, but the Duchess, whom the Duke leaves to look after the garden, did bring in eminent garden designer Arabella Lennox-Boyd. The results of the gardeners' skill and enthusiasm combined with the designer's creative flair is stunning and in places quite literally takes the breath away.

To the east the house looks over a series of immense terraces descending to a lake known as the 'Fish Pond', which was modelled by John Webb at the beginning of the nineteenth century and even today contains a good stock of fish.[3] To catch the eye on the far side of the lake is a large stone urn, beyond which the view used to continue, although it is now rather overgrown.[4] Webb had quite a hand in setting out the park, parts of which were used as an airfield during the Second World War. Immediately outside the house is a secluded terrace planted with pleached limes, scented plants,

and two very simple grass and gravel parterres. Below the walls of this terrace a luscious border in shades of blue and purple runs the length of a wide walkway. Planted here are delphiniums, agapanthus, phlox, asters and buddleias, around which dance white butterflies. A break in the colour is provided by plants such as the pale-green 'morning light' grass which, Les says, in the early frost really does live up to its name. On the other side of this walkway is another, much larger, terrace in which two *allées* of climbing rose pillars ('Felicite perpetue' and 'New Dawn') frame four yew-hedged compartments. Each compartment is themed on a different colour – pink, white, yellow and crimson – and features flowering plants such as clematis, roses, achillea and lavender as well as plenty of structured green foliage from old reliables like box and hostas. A piece of topiary in a distinct but simple shape provides the focus of each compartment, which can be enjoyed from surprisingly comfortable wooden benches guarded by urns planted in the appropriate colour. Running down the centre of this terrace, between the compartments, is a long rectangular pool, in which three jets of water play, whose clear crisp lines guide the eye forward towards the lake and the park beyond. Visible over the tops of the yew divisions are two large nineteenth-century statues by sculp-

Joan of Eaton surveys the scene in the Italian Garden.

tor Raymond Smith, one of which, 'Hunter', depicts a triumphant stallion, and the other, 'Stag at Bay', shows a man and hound battling with a stag. These have been sited here from the terrace's previous incarnations and Lennox-Boyd was apparently keen to remove them. The clients disagreed however and the statues remain, looking all the more defiant as a result.

From this terrace, curved cobbled staircases lead down to another broad gravel walk and pool, this time rectangular with curved edges, in which a battle is played out by two recent Jonathan Kenworthy sculptures of a lioness chasing a hapless beast. The final terrace, stretching down from the Broad Walk to the lake, is still waiting for its modern treatment, which is due to begin any day and will be a sleekly formal water garden planted with lines of at least a thousand trees. It has however already precipitated the removal of a stone balustrade by the lake, but wisely this was carefully photographed, documented and packed away rather than being rashly destroyed.

In the past this series of terraces has had many incarnations including formal gardens or with grass parterres, pavilions, *allées* and pools, which can be seen in an eighteenth-century engraving by Thomas Badeslade.[5] In the nineteenth century these terraces were laid out by William Andrews Nesfield, a successful designer known in particular for his ornate parterres in which gravel, grass, shrubs and flowers were used almost as a needleworker would use threads and sequins to create a piece of patterned embroidery for the garden. The *Gardener's Chronicle* described Nesfield's gardens in 1871, noting that: 'these flower-beds are admirably and perfectly kept: not a sprig of Box, leaf, flower or pebble, is out of its place; in some parts the borders are of stone, in others of Box, and the trees planted in or near the slopes, are generally Box or Yew.'[6] Photographs taken for *Country Life* magazine in 1901 show that the 'Hunter' and 'Stag at Bay' statues were used to great effect with the parterres, which are planted with helichrysum, coleus, and begonias.[7] Shortly before the First World War,

Top: Raymond Smith's 'Stag at Bay' battles amongst the modern garden compartments. Bottom: The Italian Garden boasts many spendid statues.

leading Arts and Crafts architect Detmar Blow advised on a redesign of the East Terraces to bring a fashionable simplicity in which more than 2,000 yews[8] formed tall hedges to enclose compartments on the main terrace, rather like today, in a design that H. Avray Tipping, writing for *Country Life* in 1920, saw as being a return to the eighteenth-century spirit of Eaton.[9] Photographs accompanying this 1920 article in fact show the rather plain terrace to be in a slightly sad condition, presumably because the family were not actually living there at the time.[10] Interestingly, photographs in this issue show the lowest terrace to be laid out in a design similar to that planned now, with lines of trees and a long straight pool leading towards the lake.[11]

Each end of the Broad Walk is punctuated by a garden building – a loggia and a 'Parrot House' – both of which were designed in the nineteenth-century by Alfred Waterhouse who had carried out the 3rd Marquess' revamp on the house.[12] The loggia is a discreet stone pavilion decorated only with simple carvings and displaying Roman pillars but far more dominating is the Parrot House, a round orange terracotta building raised on a terrace like a huge vibrant wedding cake. This originally contained parrots but by the time of the late Duke, contained only budgerigars, until they were released by their owner in a fit of misguided benevolence. To keep the birds in comfort, this aviary was heated with coal that travelled directly from the colliery to Eaton Hall by its private railway, the lines of which can still be seen in places.

Having undergone many transformations over their lifetime, Eaton's gardens today are still stunning not only because of the quality of their design, but also because of the excellent standard of maintenance. It is an understandable reality that in most gardens, no matter how impressive, there is usually the odd corner or two where you feel obliged to politely avert your eyes from a scruffy patch. At Eaton such corners are almost entirely absent. This has been facilitated by the effort spent in recent years in installing discreet metal strips along the edges between the grass and the paths. Whilst it is perhaps not historically authentic, this does mean that it is a simple job for Les' team to keep the paths in good shape, in turn freeing up time for the rest of the garden.

In the area behind the loggia is an enclosed herb garden, which can be enjoyed from the verandah of a pretty wooden cottage known as the Tea House, which was designed by celebrated local architect John Douglas in 1872. This building was described by the *Gardener's Chronicle* in 1884 as: 'a cottage of great cost, gabled and rustic in its plan, with all appliances for sumptuous hot-water boiling and tea-making, and a charming room for partaking of the harmless and delicious beverage.'[13] Many of the windows of this cottage are composed of tiny circular panes and Les Armstrong likes to speculate that these are the bases of wine glasses, 'perhaps broken at a wild party'! Photographs show that at the beginning of the nineteenth century this garden was very simply planted, with grass and parterres.[14] Redesigned by Arabella Lennox-Boyd, it is now planted

Right: The Parrot House is reminiscent of a wedding cake.
Opposite page nearest:
The Tea House in the herb garden.
Opposite page far right:
The gardeners' bothy once housed twenty gardeners.

with pastel-shaded roses as well as herbs such as rosemary, thyme, chives and fennel, which are used here more for their ornamental value than to supply the house. In the centre is a statue of Mercury, and watching from a small terrace in front of the Tea Cottage are two stone Talbots, traditionally the family dog. This garden is reportedly the Duchess' favourite part of Eaton Hall, and the preference is shared by Les Armstrong who appreciates this area for its quiet seclusion away from the bustle of the rest of the estate. It is ironic that in such a huge property, where the emphasis is often on impressive views and the quality of the surroundings, the occupants retreat to small, modest, enclosed areas! From here a path wends its way towards the Hall, passing a sweet wendy house and climbing frame, unusual garden features which do nevertheless remind us that Eaton is, in spite of its grandeur, a family home.

On this side, the house overlooks an Italian garden, which is so stunning as to quite literally take the breath away. Unlike that of the eastern terrace compartments, the yew hedges surrounding this area are hundreds of years old although the layout within them is more recent. The Italian garden benefited from a redesign at the end of the nineteenth century by Arts and Crafts architect Edwin Lutyens. He often collaborated with Gertrude Jekyll and later was to work on prestigious projects such as the Viceroy's Palace in New Delhi and as architect to the War Graves Commission after the First World War.[15] It was redesigned again

in 1911 by Detmar Blow, and then again by Arabella Lennox-Boyd, although a photograph from 1901 shows that the basic structure has changed very little.[16] Today, it is planted in purples and pinks using plants such as heliotrope, coleus, and petunias, which are perfectly complemented by the pinky house behind, creating an effect so hazy as to make one squint. Ornate floral beds are centred on huge mossy urns which overflow with plants, and the whole is focussed on a stone pool in which stands a Dragon Fountain created by Raymond Smith in the last years of the nineteenth-century. This scene is watched by nineteenth-century statues of medieval figures, rescued from obscurity in the park.

On the other, northern side of the house is the Spring Walk, planted mainly with spring-flowering white plants and sheltered by cherry trees. This surrounded the wooden building used in the absence of the main house and as such, as Les marvels, was once the only real garden of the now adult Duke of Westminster. This area has recently been enlarged and developed to cover the space once occupied by the temporary house.

Across the lawn from the Spring Walk is a stunning 'hot' border of exceedingly generous proportions. Originally planted in blues and whites by designer Vernon Russell Smith, Arabella Lennox-Boyd redesigned it in its current display of fiery reds and oranges, a rare sight here as the Duchess usually prefers more muted shades. Here these are thrown aside in favour of vibrant scarlet dahlias ('Bishop of

Llandaff'), *Crocosmia* 'lucifer', and 'Dublin Bay' roses, with the yellows of honeysuckle, pansies and sunflowers. This border is a great boon as it flowers from spring right through to Christmas, thanks mainly to Les Armstrong's almost religious insistence on the benefits of deadheading. Once the flowers are finished, the ornamental grasses come into their own in the frosts, having not been cut back.

Forming a backdrop to this border is the globe-topped wall of Eaton's active kitchen garden, the second currently being used as a horse paddock. Having been virtually disused for many years, this has recently been given a new

lease of life and now produces semi-organic fruit and vegetables to feed the family. As with all the best kitchen gardens, this area is beautiful as well as functional, not least because it also supplies the house with cut flowers. So many in fact, that the estate employs one lady virtually full-time to arrange them. Some of the flowers in this garden have a very virtuous function as Les practices complementary planting, growing poppies and other wildflowers near fruit in order to distract insects from the precious crop. In places the various compartments are framed by box hedges, but a particularly attractive feature is the 'stepover' apple and pear trees, in which dwarf varieties are trained to grow along knee-high railings around the various beds, to create functional yet also attractive boundaries. Just outside the kitchen garden is a picturesque bothy which is currently rented to private residents but once acted as home to no less than twenty gardeners!

The kitchen garden's recent neglect and then resurrection is only one of many such cycles in its history – in 1850 the American Frederick Law Olmsted visited Eaton whilst it was unoccupied and undergoing renovations and wrote: 'while looking for an entrance to the fruit garden, we met a gamekeeper, who was followed by a pet cub fox. He very obligingly, and with a gentlemanly manner showed us through such parts of the establishment as he was able to. There was nothing remarkable in the gardens or glasshouses, except some very large and wonderfully well-trained fruit trees on walls. Every thing was neglected now, however, and we did no more than glance at them.'[17] Only a few decades later however, Eaton had become famous for its glasshouses which were so numerous that a reporter from the *Gardener's Chronicle* in 1884 wrote that: 'The conservatories are heated by six miles of hot-water pipes; and when I asked the young fellow who had charge of myself and friends the number

Left: A knight guards the Italian Garden. Opposite page: The Camellia Walk is believed to be the longest glass corridor in the world.

of the glasshouses, he endeavoured in vain to reckon them on his fingers.'[18] These are now nowhere to be seen, having been either sold or demolished in the 1950s when the estate was in its quiet period and therefore not in need of their produce. The garden has however recently benefited from a new Victorian-style glasshouse, in which now grow delicacies such as peaches and grapes.

One survivor of the famed glasshouses is the nineteenth century Camellia Walk, which stretches along the outside of the kitchen garden. This stunning edifice, painted a bright white, is today long and thin, having lost the four limbs that once stretched from the remaining corridor, but it is still filled with camellias, many of which date from its conception, although many others are recent gifts to the Duke and Duchess. At 388 feet long, this is believed to be the longest glass corridor in the world, and so it takes a good few minutes to walk from one end to the other. Peeking through the camellias, the view from this corridor is of a terrace containing a grass lawn, where once the limbs of the glasshouse were, in which pollarded ornamental pears shield a glamorous outdoor swimming pool which brings a touch of the Riviera to Cheshire.

In comparison to the joyful displays of gardens behind the house, its setting to the front is far more restrained and even austere. The modern house, its modest proportions almost dwarfed by the neighbouring 1870s' stables, riding school and chapel clocktower, sits in the same style of forecourt as its predecessor did. The simple grass and gravel lay-out is surrounded by 350-year-old yew hedges and a low wall, and is scattered with domed golden yews. At the centre is a pool in which is a huge statue of the 1st Duke of Westminster, Hugh Lupus, on horseback. What really seizes the eye however is a stretch of fabulous golden gateway and screen in which ironwork pillars and shields, both gold and black, stretch to small grey stone pavilions with triangular roofs.

From here the double lime avenue of the

main approach stretches straight ahead as far as the Wrexham road. This can be seen, perfectly clipped, in the early eighteenth century Badeslade engraving.[19] In fact, the avenue stretches further than the eye can see because halfway down is a tall brick obelisk built in 1890 to block the view to and, more significantly, from the road. This of course was no accident – the family wanted to shield their home from the eyes of inquisitive passers-by so that today, as then, Eaton Hall remains one of Cheshire's most private houses.

A tall brick obelisk shields Eaton Hall from the road.

Alstroemercia Lutealba.

Clematis 'Ville de Lyon'.

Dahlia 'Bishop of Llandalf'.

Honeysuckle 'Dropmone Scarlet'.

Viola 'Jackanapes'.

Rose 'Swan Lake' behind Clematis 'Ville de Lyon'.

Right: Sunflower 'Taiyo'.

The loggia is used to display Roman pillars.

Select Bibliography

Acloque, Guy and Cornforth, John. 'The Eternal Gothic of Eaton - I'. *Country Life*, 11th February 1971, p304-7.

Crosby, Alan. *A History of Cheshire*. Phillimore, West Sussex, 1996.

'Eaton Hall, Chester: The Seat of The Duke of Westminster'. *Country Life*, 20th April 1901, p496-503.

English Heritage Register of Parks and Gardens of Special Historic Interest, 1999.

Gardener's Chronicle, 13th December 1884.

Gardener's Chronicle, 22nd May 1886.

Gardener's Chronicle, 3rd July 1886.

Gardener's Chronicle, 26th July 1913.

Gardener's Chronicle and Agricultural Gazette, 7th January 1871.

Gardener's Magazine, October 1831.

Laurie, Ian. 'Landscape Gardeners at Eaton Park, Chester: I. *Garden History*, Volume 12, Number 1, Spring 1984, p39-57.

Laurie, Ian. 'Landscape Gardeners at Eaton Park, Chester: II. *Garden History*, Volume 13, Number 2, Autumn 1985, p126-55.

Olmsted, Frederick. *Walks and Talks of an American Farmer in England*. George P Putnam, New York, 1852.

Outram, A. *Gardener's Chronicle*, 18th January 1896.

Tipping, H Avray. 'Eaton Hall, Cheshire: A Seat of the Duke of Westminster'. *Country Life*, 29th May 1920, p724-31.

References

1   Alan Crosby. *A History of Cheshire*. 1996, p89.
2   'Eaton Hall, Chester: The Seat of The Duke of Westminster'. *Country Life*, 20th April 1901, p496.
3   *English Heritage Register of Parks and Gardens of Special Historic Interest*, 1999.
4   'Eaton Hall, Chester: The Seat of The Duke of Westminster'. *Country Life*, 20th April 1901, p498.
5   Reproduced in Guy Acloque and John Cornforth. 'The Eternal Gothic of Eaton - I'. *Country Life*, 11th February 1971, p304.
6   *Gardener's Chronicle and Agricultural Gazette*, 7th January 1871, p14.
7   'Eaton Hall, Chester: The Seat of The Duke of Westminster'. *Country Life*, 20th April 1901, p498.
8   *Gardener's Chronicle*, 26th July 1913, p68.
9   H Avray Tipping. 'Eaton Hall, Cheshire: A Seat of the Duke of Westminster'. *Country Life*, 29th May 1920, p731.
10 H Avray Tipping. 'Eaton Hall, Cheshire: A Seat of the Duke of Westminster'. *Country Life*, 29th May 1920, p726.
11 H Avray Tipping. 'Eaton Hall, Cheshire: A Seat of the Duke of Westminster'. *Country Life*, 29th May 1920, p729.
12 *English Heritage Register of Parks and Gardens of Special Historic Interest*, 1999.
13 *Gardener's Chronicle*, 13th December 1884, p744.
14 'Eaton Hall, Chester: The Seat of The Duke of Westminster'. *Country Life*, 20th April 1901, p500.
15 *English Heritage Register of Parks and Gardens of Special Historic Interest*, 1999.
16 'Eaton Hall, Chester: The Seat of The Duke of Westminster'. *Country Life*, 20th April 1901, p496.
17 Frederick Olmsted, *Walks and Talks of an American Farmer in England*. 1852, p139.
18 *Gardener's Chronicle*, 13th December 1884, p744.
19 Reproduced in Guy Acloque and John Cornforth. 'The Eternal Gothic of Eaton - I'. *Country Life*, 11th February 1971, p304.

Arley Hall, Great Budworth

*E*veryone loves Arley Hall, so I probably ought to play Devil's Advocate and take a critical stance. Except that I too love it. As is always the way with gardens, each visitor is
able to bring their own interpretation and response, but my attachment to Arley comes from
an admiration of its having managed to carry its history, whilst maintaining a healthy enthusiasm for evolving and moving forward. This is a principle that the current owner, the 11th
Viscount Ashbrook, describes as 'preserving the best of the past, whilst still
creating new features'. In addition, Arley is quite simply a very beautiful and
atmospheric garden created not necessarily by big name designers, but by a
succession of owners because, as Lord Ashbrook says, 'each generation has
been interested and keen about gardening'.

Arley became home to the Warburton family in the fifteenth century,
although they had owned it for some centuries before that.[1] In the
eighteenth century it was inherited by Sir Peter Warburton, the fourth
baronet, and during his lifetime the house, pleasure grounds and
a walled kitchen garden developed, and the landscape park
was laid out.[2] The fifth baronet, also Sir Peter, enlarged the
park and brought in William Emes, who had already carried
out a small amount of work on the large lawn and ha-ha to the
south of the house, to produce a plan for the park and gardens.[3] This park is still relatively intact today, and is still in the
same ownership as the house, although the land is on a grazing let.

At the time of the park's creation, the main gardens were to the east
of the house, the famous compartments of today were largely orchards
and productive kitchen gardens, with the main pleasure gardens being
to the east.[4] William Emes' 1785 plan of the proposed park shows the
eastern gardens as consisting of curving flowerbeds with sinuous paths
with an area lightly planted with trees and winding walkways further
away from the house. The flower garden is long since gone, but the
current Lord and Lady Ashbrook (the Ashbrook name was introduced

Top: Arley Hall looks out over a magnificent park.
Inset: A youthful statue adorns the Flag Garden.

The Rootree pond is verdant & atmospheric.

Although largely ornamental, the Kitchen Garden still has a traditional feel.

A Lime avenue & Salvin clocktower welcome the visitors.

The 'Fish Garden' no longer contains any fish, after they were stolen by herons.

to Arley's history when Elizabeth Egerton-Warburton, the current owner's mother, inherited the property from her father, and married the 10th Viscount Ashbrook) have invested their energies into clearing the undergrowth and dense rhododendron plantings that had amassed beyond here, and planting many new trees ranging from oaks to acers and shrubs such as pieris and kalmia. Thus the Grove area with its winding walkways has been reintroduced, with a Woodland Walk beyond it.

In the nineteenth century, Arley passed to Rowland Egerton-Warburton (who was one of the Egertons of Oulton Park). Rowland and his wife Mary had the house rebuilt to more or less its present appearance by local architect George Latham, who also built the low wall today marking the Emes' ha-ha. They also began to develop the area to the west of the house as pleasure gardens, although the walled kitchen gardens would of course have been continued in order to supply the house with food.

As a tourist attraction Arley now boasts 30,000 visitors annually (excluding the guests at its forty or fifty weddings and numerous other events). These bring in the money to enable its gardens to be maintained at a higher standard than is customary in most twenty-first-century homes. The gardens that attract these visitors are largely those created by Rowland and Mary, as the basic structure they imposed has changed very little since their lifetime.

The approach is by an unassuming estate road rather than by a grand drive so the visitor feels rather as though he is sneaking up on Arley, but a proper welcome is finally given by a smart parade of pleached limes that Rowland Egerton-Warburton planted to lead to a courtyard

of stables and fifteenth-century barn, as well as a folksy wooden clocktower which was designed in the nineteenth-century by Anthony Salvin, who is also responsible for the chapel that stands to the east of the house.

Today's paying visitor is encouraged to enter the gardens by turning right just beyond the courtyard, rather than the more dramatic entry from the house, which is via the 201-metre-long gravel Furlong Walk, which shields the gardens from the park. This is today planted with a fine display of rhododendrons, which after the First World War replaced the original plantings of formally-clipped hollies, aucuba, ilex and yew which can be seen in a photograph from *Country Life* magazine of 1904.[5] Even today though, the visitor has a delicious feeling of knowing that hidden delights wait behind the rhododendrons. Just beyond the courtyard the visitor enters the veritable maze of gardens. Starting from the courtyard entrance, the first of these delights is small, understated compartments, and there is a tendency to rush past in anticipation of more lush scenes to come. Here are the Herb Garden, Scented Garden and Flag Garden. The latter gets its name from its stone flags, and was created in 1900 by Antoinette Egerton-Warburton, the daughter-in-law of Rowland and Mary.[6] Here, geometric beds are planted with lavender and roses, and scarlet tropaeolum scrambles through the yew. The honeycomb system of 'rooms' means that there tends to be no prescribed way to move around Arley, but from these initial compartments a hedged path joins with the Furlong Walk, which provides a pleasant walk between the park and the rhododendrons before giving way to Arley's most famous view, indeed, one of England's most famous garden views. This is the Herbaceous Border, often claimed in fact to be England's first. Writing in 1904 in *Some English Gardens*, the book she published with watercolourist George S. Elgood, the influential Edwardian designer Gertrude Jekyll was unreserved in her admiration of this area: 'Throughout the length and breadth of England it would be hard to

The Sundial Garden boasts a pair of urns from the Marbury estate.

find borders of hardy flowers handsomer or in any way better done than those at Arley in Cheshire.'[7] A sunny grass alley, originally gravel, leads up through the centre of two wide borders, which George Elgood's ultra-pretty watercolour shows to have been planted with flowering plants such as blue delphiniums, white and orange lilies, and orange poppies. These are punctuated with sculpted yew buttresses and enclosed on one side by a tall yew hedge and on the other by a soft red brick wall. Jekyll is very clear on the value of yew in such schemes, as its forms 'take that distinct light and shade, and strong variations of solidity of green colouring, that make the surfaces of our clipped English yew so valuable a ground work for masses of brilliant flowers.'[8] At the end of the walk is a graceful stone alcove seat

from the eighteenth century, from which the view down the border ends in a rustic view of the park and grazing sheep. Gertrude Jekyll described this view: 'From this walk there is a very beautiful view across the steeply-falling gradient of the park to the lake. The park has grand old oak trees that fall into picturesque groups. Beyond the lake again are fine masses of timber. The lake is a sheet of water that takes a winding course and disappears among the trees.'[9] The shape of this lake can still be made

Top: The Tea Cottage was once used for parties. Middle: The Ilex Avenue is one of Arley's most distinctive features. Bottom: A gateway leads from the herbaceous border to the Walled Garden.

out, but the water has long since disappeared. It would be good to be able to reinstate this feature, but at the moment the bureaucracy involved in such a change is great. In spring this view is made almost too delightful by the arrival of lambs! Just in front of the alcove, there are two exits out of the Herbaceous Border: to the left a break in the yew hedge leads to an Ilex Avenue and further garden compartments, and to the right a grand Victorian gateway leads to two walled gardens.

The Ilex Avenue was planted in the mid-nineteenth century and is today a mature and dignified avenue, albeit a short one, in which fourteen cylindrically clipped holm oaks, *Quercus ilex*, lead the eye out towards the park. After the Herbaceous Border, the Ilex Avenue is Arley's signature feature. It is ironic therefore that in his correspondence with his brother-in-law Rowland Egerton-Warburton, James Bateman, the creator of the celebrated Biddulph Grange gardens just outside the Cheshire borders in Staffordshire, was critical

of Rowland's choice: 'I don't like your ilexes and would strongly recommend you to substitute Cembra Pines which are of the easiest culture, perfectly hardy, and of a most dignified aspect … You can't make ilexes grow equally together and they don't like the knife'.[10] In fact though, in Bateman's day these trees would not have been quite so distinctive – photographs in *Country Life* show them to have originally been the typical cone shape, embellished with small domed yews at their feet, and it was only after they were neglected during the First World War that they had to be developed into today's distinctive cylinders.[11] Certainly, Gertrude Jekyll recognised the demands of such formal clipping, writing in *Some English Gardens* of the maze that was once in this corner of the Arley gardens: 'The maze should not be forgotten. It is at the back of the alcove and the bowling-green. These old garden toys are very seldom planted now. Perhaps people have not time for them. Also they are costly of labour; the area of green wall of a maze of even moderate size, that has to be clipped yearly,

if computed would amount to an astonishing figure.'[12]

Along with the maze, the bowling green mentioned by Jekyll has since disappeared, having been replaced partly by a tennis court which is visible in unappealing glimpses through the Ilex Avenue, but more successfully by an open, pleasant and polite 'Fish Garden'. This was so named because it used to contain goldfish but this habit was abandoned in the face of adversity from herons. This sunken garden is held by low mossy walls and has a small square pool decorated with sunny forget-me-nots and diminutive domed yews. It is watched over by a solemn row of gravestones that belong to Rowland Egerton-Warburton's horses and boast affectionate engravings from their master, such as this to a horse named

Saltfish:
'For hungry Worms here lies a noble Dish,
Horseflesh by Nature and by Name Saltfish',
and this to Miss Miggs:
'Brood Mare so Faultless none will e'er see more
Her only rivals were the Stocks she bore
From her six Fillies and eight Colts were Bred
Some matchless Hunters many a Gallop led
Of Arley stable each in turn the Pride
While each in turn it was a joy to ride.'
At the end of the Ilex Avenue is a view of the park across an invisible ha-ha. This is surely one of the most successful to be seen today, as even the wise and 'special effect' orientated twenty-first-century viewer can be tricked into

*Opposite: Arley is filled with beautiful flowers likes verbenas (top),
passion flowers (middle) & roses (bottom). This page above: It is a
springtime treat to see the Herbaceous Border coming to life.
Below: An arbour from Durrow ornaments the Kitchen Garden.*

thinking the sheep are superbly trained not to come into the garden, rather than being restrained by the hidden ditch. Steps lead down towards the park view from the Ilexes and into a tucked away lawn area known as the Sundial Garden, which is decorated with yellow and orange azaleas and pinky-mauve hydrangeas. On either side are eighteenth-century stone urns which were brought here from Marbury Hall, a nearby country estate which was demolished in the 1970s having been requisitioned in the Second World War, then bought and demolished by a property developer, before being rented as a country park by the local council.

The west side of the Sundial Garden leads to the intriguingly named 'Rootree'. This area was created by Rowland and Mary as an alpine rock garden[13] but has since grown into a rather shady nook so that the emphasis has to be on its more verdant plants like hostas and ferns, including the original 'Royal Fern' (*Osmunda regalis*), as well as rhododendrons. Essentially a sunken rock garden with a small pool running through it, the Rootree has earned its name from a small brick cave hidden in one of its banks. This would originally have looked almost like something built by goblins rather than the man-made feature it really was, being covered with decorative tree stumps and roots, some of which survive.

To the other side of the Ilex Avenue is an area planted with lawns and shrub rose beds in an informal style, although it was originally more structured, with topiary and geometric circular and square beds.[14] The focus of this corner is the Tea Cottage, a tiny brick building with black and white timbering, so called because it was used for tea parties.[15]

These garden compartments to the west of the Herbaceous Border were largely laid-out in the nineteenth century by Rowland and Mary, but those within the two walled gardens to the east of the border have been the work of the current Lord Ashbrook's mother, followed by his wife from the 1960s onwards. The first, which is known simply as the Walled Garden, ceased to be a traditional kitchen garden during the Second World War when it was used as a market garden, before then becoming dedicated to pleasure. Today it has at its centre four Dawyck beech trees and a quatrefoil pool, guarded by small weather-worn statues of heraldic beasts, which were once on the roof of the house. Four paths lead out from this, and so effectively quarter the enclosure. The design is simple and relies on the immense beds of shrubs and herbaceous plants that line each of the four walls, with the remainder being left as immaculate lawn.

From here, a gate leads to the Kitchen Garden, on the wall of which is a long Victorian vinery which still produces figs from its original plants. Around the garden are beds of fruit and vegetables, which are eaten largely by the Ashbrook family. The focus of this garden is however increasingly ornamental, having been developed in the last years of the twentieth century. At the centre is a nostalgic pleasure garden feature in which a white arbour sits at the end of a short walk through borders of lavender, tulips and box. This arbour looks like the birdcages found in North African doorways, but in fact was brought from Castle Durrow in Ireland, the Ashbrooks' ancestral home.

The final garden to have undergone changes in recent years is that on the eastern front of the Hall, where a William Andrews Nesfield terrace was set out in 1850. The plan for this is still held at Arley Hall and reveals a great deal about how this terrace would have looked. Nesfield writes: 'Central grass plot having a mound/raised one foot, surmounted by a gilded globe Dial, or some other conspicuously large sculpture object (the point d'affini of the whole) – minor vases, with pedestals on grass circles, at the angles of the three compartments, (similar in size, because they are not only arranged quincunx with their respective centres, but act as symmetrical sentinels on the main flanking walks'.[16] The largest sculpture was surrounded by 'three subcompartments of embroidered Beds, edged with Box upon white gravel or ground Pottery "Saggers" for the lowest kind of Flowers in masses of one colour'. The end of the terrace nearest the park was reserved for tall flowers, and the whole was planted with lines of shrubs including *Ulex stricta*, *Abies pigmea*, *Juniperus communis stricta* and *Arborvitae* (chinese), and dotted with *Auracaria imbracata*, *Yucca floriasa*, and *Juniperus excelsa*. Stretching out from the house to the park was a 'row of standard roses', each in 'pebbled circles' and trimmed into a neat umbrella shape.[17] *Country Life* photographs of 1904 show this arrangement to have been very beautiful, like a piece of fine embroidery thrown over the English countryside.[18] Unfortunately, this area was ploughed up and the stone vases destroyed so that it could be used as a football pitch during the Second World War when Arley was a convalescent home for servicemen. Today the terrace is still balustraded with a view over the park, but is planted as the private garden of Mr and Mrs Charles Foster (sister and brother-in-law of Lord Ashbrook), who live in a flat within the main hall.

It is glimpses such as this of Mr and Mrs Foster's garden that reminds us, with a jolt, that Arley is still a family home, in spite of its thousands of visitors. This though is a home like no other, rather it must be one of the hardest working residences around. On their succession, Lord and Lady Ashbrook did not want to live in the main Hall but they do nevertheless live just outside the Lime Avenue in the Arley Parsonage. Do not think however that the buildings at Arley are allowed to go empty. The Fosters live in a flat in the Hall, and the modern but matching courtyard to the east consists of private family homes which were built and sold a few years ago to raise money for Arley. These occupy the site of an unmanageable wing of the old Hall which was demolished in 1968 because of the impossible cost of maintaining the already decaying building, but after the demolition it became horribly clear that in fact the remaining structure looked incomplete without the other part. Viscount Ashbrook has led 'another life' practising law but nevertheless it is fair to say that running his home as a visitor attraction is a full-time job, involving many staff as well as the family's energies. As I walk round their gardens, I silently thank them for taking the trouble.

Left: The entrance to the Herbaceous Border is full of excitement.
Right: The Furlong Walk is now planted with rhododendrons
but was once a display of topiary.

Select Bibliography

Ashbrook, Elizabeth. *The Story of a Garden, Arley 1831-1991*. Arley Hall Press, Northwich, 1991.
Ashbrook, Michael; Ashbrook, Elizabeth; and Foster, Charles. *Arley Hall and Gardens, Cheshire*, Jarrold Publishing, Norwich, 1999.
'Arley Hall, Cheshire: The Residence of Mr Piers Egerton-Warburton'. *Country Life*, 24th December 1904, p942-50.
Elgood, George S and Jekyll, Gertrude. *Some English Gardens*. Longmans, Green and Co., London, 1904.
English Heritage Register of Parks and Gardens of Special Historic Interest, 1999.
Foster, Charles. 'A History of the Gardens at Arley Hall, Cheshire'. *Garden History*, Volume 24, Number 2, Winter 1996, p255-271.

References

The archive material used is held at Arley Hall.

1   *English Heritage Register of Parks and Gardens of Special Historic Interest*, 1999.
2   Charles Foster. 'A History of the Gardens at Arley Hall, Cheshire'. *Garden History*, Volume 24, Number 2, Winter 1996, p260.
3   Charles Foster. 'A History of the Gardens at Arley Hall, Cheshire'. *Garden History*, Volume 24, Number 2, Winter 1996, p262.
4   William Emes 'Plan for the park at Arley Hall', 1785.
5   'Arley Hall, Cheshire: The Residence of Mr Piers Egerton-Warburton'. *Country Life*, 24th December 1904, p947.
6   Michael Ashbrook, Elizabeth Ashbrook and Charles Foster. *Arley Hall and Gardens, Cheshire*. 1999, p26.
7   George S Elgood and Gertrude Jekyll. *Some English Gardens*. 1904, p125.
8   George S Elgood and Gertrude Jekyll. *Some English Gardens*. 1904, p125.
9   George S Elgood and Gertrude Jekyll. *Some English Gardens*. 1904, p127.
10 Letter from James Bateman, 1858, held at Arley Hall.
11 *Arley Hall and Gardens, Cheshire*. 1999, p30.
12 George S Elgood and Gertrude Jekyll. *Some English Gardens*. 1904, p127.
13 Michael Ashbrook, Elizabeth Ashbrook and Charles Foster. *Arley Hall and Gardens, Cheshire*. 1999, p32.
14 Painting of 'The Rose Garden, Arley'. George S Elgood and Gertrude Jekyll. *Some English Gardens*. 1904.
15 Michael Ashbrook, Elizabeth Ashbrook and Charles Foster. *Arley Hall and Gardens, Cheshire*, 1999, p29.
16 WA Nesfield. 'Detailed Plan of proposed Parterre for Arley Hall', 1846.
17 WA Nesfield. 'Detailed Plan of proposed Parterre for Arley Hall', 1846.
18 'Arley Hall, Cheshire: The Residence of Mr Piers Egerton-Warburton'. *Country Life*, 24th December 1904, p946.

Crewe Hall, Crewe

Crewe Hall is today not one of the sites to immediately spring to mind as a 'great garden of Cheshire', as its splendid gothic hall sits in unremarkable surroundings consisting of forecourt-cum-car park, light industrial area, walled garden-cum-football pitch, and commercial woodland. This sorry landscape evolved during the twentieth century when Crewe Hall was used first as an army base, and then as the offices of the Wellcome Foundation (previously Calmic), before today hopefully seeing brighter days as a hotel. In a previous life however, it boasted gardens that were amongst the finest in the country, let alone the county.

Crewe Hall is mentioned in the Domesday Book as being the property of Richard de Vernon, Baron of Shipbroke.[1] It passed then through several hands and families until it was bought in the late sixteenth century by Sir Randulph Crewe, later to be Lord Chief Justice. In 1615 Randulph Crewe began the construction of a noteworthy mansion, of which seventeenth-century historian Thomas Fuller said 'Sir Randal first brought the Model of excellent Building into these remoter parts; yea, brought London into Cheshire in the Loftiness, Sightliness and Pleasantness of their Structures'.[2] The great Cheshire historian George Ormerod wrote in 1819 that: 'From a painting preserved at Crewe, it [Sir Randulph's house] appears in its original state to have been surrounded with offices and square courts and gardens, built in a style corresponding with the house, and laid out in trim parterres, according to the fashion of the day.'[3] To the west of the Hall today are still brick stables with a distinctive horse head decoration that date from this time, although the tall chimney was added in the

Top: Sir Randulph Crewe's hall, as illustrated in George Ormerod's 'The History of the County Palatine and City of Chester'.
Inset: Heraldic beasts embellish the north terrace.

nineteenth-century.[4] The Apple Store, a small octagonal brick building with the look of a pigeonhouse to the west of the Hall, is also of the same period and is linked via a tunnel to the huge walled kitchen garden whose dimensions of 140 by 80 metres make it a useful home to a local football club. Vegetables and cutting flowers would of course be preferable occupants, but at least its red brick walls do survive, which is more than can be said for the orchard which had sat to the north of the walled garden, before being sacrificed to a Wellcome Corporation cricket pitch in the twentieth century. The kitchen garden survived in full-use until the twentieth century and in 1892 the *Gardener's Chronicle* published an article about a visit to Crewe Hall in which the author devoted many paragraphs to it: 'here I cannot refrain from writing in the first person, in order to say that I have seldom, if ever, enjoyed a stroll through glass-houses as I did under Mr. Whitaker's [the head gardener] guidance. His wide knowledge of plants, and his evident fondness for everything under his charge, made me realise how he had grown to a Gladstonian old age in his master's service. As he said himself, "Lord Crewe and I have grown old together."[5] This invaluable article goes on to describe the growing of peaches, camellias, melons, 'Splendid luscious Figs', pineapples, and Todea and Killarney ferns.

In the seventeenth century Crewe Hall was transferred by marriage to John Offley of Madeley, Staffordshire. This gentleman's son in turn inherited the property and reverted to the name of Crewe. His grandson, who was created Baron Crewe of Crewe in 1806, enlarged the house and put a great deal of energy into the estate, which now had a Repton and Emes landscape park rather than the previous formal gardens to the north of the house. Humphry Repton produced designs for the park and, with typical confidence, was rather scathing when describing his impressions of Crewe as he found it: 'In judging the character of any place to which I am a stranger, I very minutely observe the first impression it makes up on my mind, and, comparing it with subsequent impressions, I inquire into the causes which may have rendered my first judgment erroneous. I confess there has hardly occurred to me an instance where I have experienced so great a fluctuation of opinion as in this place. I was led, from a consideration of the antiquity of the Crewe family in Cheshire, to expect a certain degree of magnificence; but my first view of the house being from an unfavourable point, and at too great a distance to judge of its real magnitude, I conceived it to be very small; and measuring the surrounding objects by this false standard, the whole place lost that importance which I afterwards found it assume on a closer examination ... When we formerly approached the mansion through a village of its poor dependants, we were not offended at their proximity, because the massy gates and

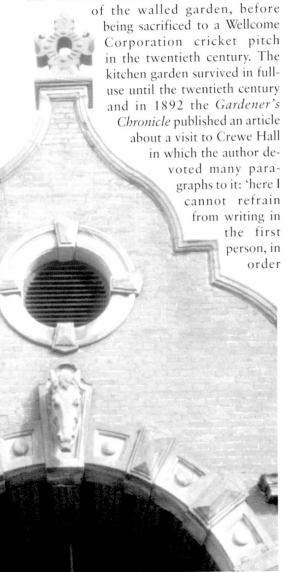

The ornate entrance to the surviving seventeenth-century stable block.

numerous courts sufficiently marked the distance betwixt the palace and the cottage: these being removed, other expedients must be adopted to restore the native character of Crewe Hall.'[6]

Writing in 1819, Ormerod is highly complimentary about the Crewe Hall as honed by Baron Crewe, which he would have been able to see first-hand: 'there can certainly be none ['buildings in the kingdom'] more indebted to their proprietors for preserving the original style unaltered, and for the manner in which the antient fabric has been made to groupe with modern landscape.'[7] In Ormerod's great historical tome is an engraving of Crewe Hall at this time, showing the open grass of the park to lead directly from the naturalistic lake to the house.[8]

The third Baron, Hungerford Crewe, saw the place at its most bold. During this period, a terrace to the east of the hall was set out, which now looks out over a small industrial park but is still bordered with a balustrade guarded by stone beasts. It passes round the side of the house to the north and from here today overlooks a plain grassed sloping area. This is enclosed by a beech hedge and has a rectangular twentieth-century pool at the far end, as well as an early nineteenth-century spiral stone sundial. In the nineteenth-century however this area would have been absolutely stunning, having been laid out by William Andrews Nesfield in around 1860. The project must have been considered an important one by Nesfield, as the John Rylands Library in Manchester holds a great deal of correspondence between Nesfield, Lord Crewe, Head Gardener Mr Whitaker, and EH Martin, Lord Crewe's lawyer.[9] Clearly, Nesfield and Whitaker were working in close contact, as is demonstrated by a fascinating sequence of letters between them. In the first, Nesfield wrote to Lord Crewe to tell him that 'I will duly attend to your Lordship's instructions regarding Wellingtonias and should say Guinea plants will be quite sufficient money to spend as they grow rapidly and if properly planted (which I will give instructions for) will soon be effective' (27th January 1862). Whitaker then informed EH Martin that 'I am writing today by his Lordship's directions, to Mr Nesfield, asking him to secure Wellingtonia plants by the time they will be wanted in the autumn' (21st February 1862) and Nesfield then wrote to Lord Crewe to inform him that 'Your instructions regarding the Wellingtonias shall be duly attended to immediately and I have no doubt that in the case of Whitaker (who understands his business so admirably) the plants will improve by the time the ground is ready to receive them' (22nd February 1862). In the same letter, Nesfield also expressed confidence in Mr Merton, the contractor employed to carry out the work: 'He is a remarkably attentive man and I feel certain the work when finished will give your Lordship satisfaction.'

Photographs from *Country Life* in 1902 show the result to have been an awe-inspiring arrangement of parterres leading to a sweeping view across a lake to woodland beyond. The author of the accompanying article is congratulatory on the success of the scene: 'The terrace work, with the grotesque animals to give point and character, is singularly beautiful, and it will be observed that excellent sculpture holds a right place here. The sundial is an admirable example of a true garden ornament, telling fleeting hours by the sun. The outlook from the terrace over the lake has a particular charm of its own. There is formality in the regular shapes of the bedding, and some may quarrel with the characters; but let us recognise that there is merit in this style as any other. Here, at least, are design and colour in sharp and definite form, making a foreground

An urn is one of the few embellishments of the north garden today.

beyond which the placid lake and long belts of glorious trees seem to derive new beauties.'[10] The *Gardener's Chronicle* also extolled this view, writing in 1892: 'the flower-bedding, well done as it was, was only a minor factor in the landscape. For from the very start the beautiful natural curving of the outline of the lake, gleaming in the dip below, had been in full view. The opposite side of the lake is wooded with openings in places; to the right there is a pretty verdurous island, beyond which the park of 600 acres undulates away into the far distance. Thus in this flower garden one can stand amidst

Contrasting a naturalistic, picturesque view with an overtly designed parterre was a key part of Nesfield's style, reflecting the Victorian preference for viewing the natural landscape from a more refined standpoint. This view is also now lost along with the parterre, as the lake was drained in 1941 after the dam gave way,[12] and at the end of garden instead is a wall of poplars. This is one of several areas of commercial planting currently occupying the northern part of the park, including Temple of Peace Wood, the wooded area originally viewed on the lake's far bank. The roof of the lake's

pretty surroundings, and gaze long and lovingly on a beautiful natural scene. The walk round the lake, too, is very well worth taking. In the twilight, often in the hush of Nature, there is an absolute stillness of the water very provocative of romantic dreams and fancies. That the Crewe family have felt this charm is proved by a temple in a grove of trees being called "The Temple of Peace".'[11]

boathouse jutted over the water and was used as a terrace with a statue of Neptune and a nymph for decoration. It still exists today, hidden amongst the trees, although Neptune looks rather sad without his watery view.

Sadly, a serious fire meant that in 1866 the 3rd Baron had to rebuild the house, which his father had restored and improved in the 1830s. According to *Country Life* in 1902, he coped

This page: Some of Crewe Hall's fine details do still survive.

Above: A 1902 Country Life *photograph shows the WA Nesfield parterre & ornamental lake to the north of the house (Country Life Picture Library). Below: The scene to the north of the house today.*

admirably with the situation however, it being reported that he 'was a man of great *sang froid*, and that, while his ancient home was in flames, he ordered a table to be placed on the lawn, and then and there wrote a telegram for his architect: "Crewe is burning; come and build it up again."'[13] This architect was in fact Edward Barry, son of Charles, who had designed the very grand Charing Cross railway station. The work done was mainly on the interior, although in a letter dated 25th January 1875, Barry does refer to a bill of £210 'For preparing several designs and estimates for forecourt, Iron Gates … according to plans now abandoned also for designs and estimates of Conservatory and Greenhouses'.[14]

After this though, the estate was never to see such glory days again as it passed to Baron Crewe's nephew, Lord Houghton, who in the 1930s sold a large part of it to the Duchy of Lancaster. The Hall was used by the war department during the Second World War and housed American and Australian troops, as well as 2,000 German prisoners of war. After this, it was leased by the medical company Calmic, later to be taken over by the Wellcome Corporation. As the twentieth century edged to a close, a new future was in the offing for Crewe Hall as it was spotted by Philip Humphries, a businessman with a passion for taking historic properties and making them work in the modern age. Having fallen in love with Crewe Hall he successfully persuaded the Duchy of Lancaster to sell the still fantastic Hall and its immediate grounds to him in 1998.

Spending millions of pounds on the property's fabric, Humphries now operates it as a successful hotel with the mission of offering the general public an opportunity to visit a stunning stately home without having to leave at five o'clock when the gates shut. The luxury hotel attracts around 170 weddings each year, a figure which will surely only be helped by Humphries' plans to gradually restore the

A fine terrace still stretches around Crewe Hall.

garden to the north of the house, returning Nesfield's *fleur de lis* to pride of place. Sadly though, any further landscape restoration would be a huge project and must be rather limited by the commercial planting that fills the Reptonian lake, and the presence of the industrial estate which curtails the garden to the east. We can all breathe a sigh of relief that Crewe Hall still exists at all, but it sadly seems as though only a miracle could return its gardens to the beauty in which they once revelled.

Select Bibliography

'Crewe Hall, Cheshire, A Seat of the Earl of Crewe'. *Country Life*, 29th March 1902, p400-8.
'Crewe Hall, Cheshire, The Seat of the Marquess of Crewe'. *Country Life*, 3rd May 1913, p634-40.
de Figueiredo, Peter and Treuherz, Julian. *Cheshire County Houses*. Phillimore, Sussex, 1988.
English Heritage Register of Parks and Gardens of Special Historic Interest, 1999.
Fuller, Thomas. *The History of the Worthies of England*. J.G.W.L and W.G., London, 1662.
Gardener's Chronicle, 17th December 1892.
Gardener's Chronicle, 4th December 1880.
Gardener's Chronicle and Agricultural Gazette, 7th February 1863.
Harris, John. *The Artist and the Country House, from the Fifteenth Century to the Present Day*, Sotheby Pathe Bernet Publications, London, 1979.
Laurie, Ian. 'Nesfield in Cheshire'. *Garden History*, Volume 15, Number 2, 1987, p145-155.
Ormerod, George. *The History of the County Palatine and City of Chester*. Volume 3, Lackington, Hughes, Harding, Mavor, and Jones, London, 1819.
Repton, Humphry. *Sketches and Hints on Landscape Gardening*. W. Bulmer and Co., London, 1794.

The archive material used is held at the John Rylands Library (Roundell Muniments) and in the Cheshire Record Office.

References

[1] 'Crewe Hall, Cheshire, A Seat of the Earl of Crewe'. *Country Life*, 29th March 1902, p400.
[2] Thomas Fuller. *The History of the Worthies of England*. 1662, p178.
[3] George Ormerod. *The History of the County Palatine and City of Chester*. Volume 3, 1819, p168.
[4] *English Heritage of Parks and Gardens of Special Historic Interest*, 1999.
[5] *Gardener's Chronicle*, 17th December 1892, p741.
[6] Humphry Repton. *Sketches and Hints on Landscape Gardening*. 1794, p7.
[7] George Ormerod. *The History of the County Palatine and City of Chester*. Volume 3, 1819, p168.
[8] George Ormerod. *The History of the County Palatine and City of Chester*. Volume 3, 1819, p168.
[9] John Rylands Library Roundell Muniments, I Deeds and Allied Documents, Chester, Dorfold, Wilbraham Spencer Tollemache.
[10] 'Crewe Hall, Cheshire, A Seat of the Earl of Crewe'. *Country Life*, 29th March 1902, p408.
[11] *Gardener's Chronicle*, 17th December 1892, p740.
[12] *English Heritage of Parks and Gardens of Special Historic Interest*, 1999.
[13] 'Crewe Hall, Cheshire, A Seat of the Earl of Crewe'. *Country Life*, 29th March 1902, p407.
[14] Cheshire Record Office DCR15/7 EM Barrie Correspondence 1866-79.

Dorfold Hall, Nantwich

T he atmosphere at Dorfold Hall near Nantwich is very much that of a garden enjoying a quiet period of its life. There is not, fortunately, the sense of one whose features are being left to decay, but nor is there the urgent bustle of a high-maintenance garden filled with new projects in order to satisfy eager visitors. It has not always been like this though – in the nineteenth century it benefitted from the touch of one of the best Victorian garden designers available.

Having belonged to the Wilbraham family since the beginning of the seventeenth century, Dorfold was bought in 1754 by James Tomkinson, a rich Bostock lawyer. It was James' grandson, the Reverend James, who set in motion what was to be the most significant garden development at Dorfold, asking WA Nesfield to draw-up designs for the gardens. At this stage however they remained unimplemented, it is said because Mrs Tomkinson opposed the plans.[1] However, the Reverend's daughter Ann and her husband Wilbraham Spencer Tollemache inherited Dorfold in 1861 and Tollemache wasted no time in calling on Nesfield again – by November he was writing of drinking tea with the designer at the Hall (25th November 1861).[2] This time however, the designs were actually carried out and Nesfield's involvement is now one of the remaining gardens' most precious attributes. Having taken the plunge, Tollemache at least was pleased with the results, leading Nesfield to write: 'I promised Mr T. to give Dorfold a look which I am very glad to learn does not disappoint as to effect - wait a bit longer however till it is all green and tidy.' (10th March 1862)[3]

Nesfield introduced the double lime avenue that today frames the low red-brick house on the approach, although this is now rather spoilt by nasty broken tarmac. At the end is a lilied-fish pond, the end of which was in fact filled in by Nesfield, who wrote of having

*Top: Dorfold's main garden is still pretty, despite the loss of W A Nesfield's parterre.
Inset: A mastiff puppy & siblings sit in the forecourt.*

Dorfold's cast iron mastiff statue is said to have come from the 1855 Paris Exhibition.

Dorfold rejoices in its floral borders.

The woodland garden is crammed with relaxed plantings.

A green pool meanders through the woodland garden.

sufficient earth to fill in the 'hungry ponds' (2nd November 1861).[4] Even at this stage his involvement did not go entirely smoothly and whilst his designs were being implemented there was an anxious exchange of letters between him, Mr Tollemache, and the Dorfold solicitor, EH Martin, when it was discovered that they had misinterpreted his plans. Nesfield was exasperated by this confusion, writing: 'the principle of my operation is so simple that I cannot see how anything more should be misunderstand.'(2nd November 1861)[5] We tend to think that our generation invented the super-hurried 'Groundforce' approach to garden making, but Nesfield's letter seems to be written in great haste, suggesting that work on the approach was racing ahead. To add to his panic, a little note is scrawled on the outside of his letter to say that there would be a delay in its delivery as 'I find the plan is too late for Book post, viz after 4pm'. As he said, 'This is unlucky'.

The avenue ends at a picture-perfect forecourt with turning circle, in which the ground is decorated with grey and white cobbles in swirling patterns every bit as ornate as Nesfield's parterres. This is surrounded on three sides by mellow red brick buildings. To the north is the main house, much of which dates from the ownership of Ralph Wilbraham in the early seventeenth century. To the east and west are fiddly arrangements of buildings, in which the original pavilions at the front of the forecourt were attached to the house in the nineteenth century. The pavilions are draped with climbing roses and their wings each have tiny windows and wooden doors with arched gables in a way that is strangely reminiscent of chess pieces. Writing in 1848 SC Hall described the visual success of this arrangement of buildings: 'The front of Dorfold is highly picturesque. The two small lodges seen in front belong to the original construction; but modern domestic arrangements requiring more room than was afforded by the old building, the small offices between the house and the old lodges have been

The forecourt is framed by intricate buildings.

added.'[6] At the centre of the turning circle is a large iron statue of a mastiff and her suckling young, said to have come from the Paris Exhibition of 1855, which had been inspired by Prince Albert's Great Exhibition a few years earlier.[7] To either side are grass edges with a sizeable clipped yew, almost as tall as the buildings behind, with lower yew rings around their base, although photographs accompanying a 1904 *Country Life* article shows that these were once trimmed into three distinct rings.[8]

To the south of the house we can enter the gardens by a wooden ivy-trailed door, feeling very much like a character in Francis Hodgson Burnett's *The Secret Garden*. Through the door however is not Hodgson Burnett's overgrown jungle, but rather a pleasant low-walled lawn where once rested Nesfield's other main contribution to Dorfold, one of his famous parterres. This, like so many of its kind, was lost when the Second World War swallowed-up resources but in spite of this, the South Lawn is still a very attractive scene, lined with herbaceous borders in gentle pastel shades. Photographs of this area were shown in an article for *Country Life* magazine in 1908 and it was then laid out as Nesfield had intended with a gravel path encircling parterre plantings of tulips, punctuated with small cones and domes of box.[9] Steps from this top lawn cut through the wall and lead down to another, plain and smooth lawn, which looks out into the parkland. Although there are more impressive parks to be seen, this particular view is an especially peaceful one as the long grass slopes away, eventually down to a fish pond. The *Country Life* writer of 1908 was certainly impressed by the park here, although he was slightly disparaging about the Cheshire topography: 'This part of Cheshire is decidedly flat, but there are pleasant undulations and stretches of water in Dorfold Park, and the variety, grouping and size of the timber lend it picturesqueness and distinction.'[10] To the left the scene is bounded by a red brick wall, and in an alcove here none other than William Shakespeare catches the eye – this near-lifesize statue is not as incongruous as might first appear, as it serves as a reminder that Dorfold was first built in the same year that he died (1616). The bard is accompanied by four white standard rose bushes, rather like a popstar with his groupies.

To the right the South Lawn is again bounded by a walled garden. This wall is backdrop to a deep herbaceous border, divided by clipped yew blocks, reminiscent of those at Arley. The South Lawn eventually stretches around the side of the house, where it is shaded by an immense oak tree. It is worth exploring this area as the tree's canopy shields two treasures. One is a seventeenth-century stone gateway, now sadly looking out only to a scruffy track through overgrown woodland, that was taken from a now demolished building in Nantwich.[11] This squat but ornate gateway features stone lions on top and in niches on either side, the busts of King James I and his wife Queen Anne, said to be later additions again to indicate the period of Dorfold's construction.[12] The other treasure is an amusing surprise: a plain stone urn boasts what appears to be a resplendent aloe, unexpectedly thriving in such a shady spot, but when the visitor is drawn nearer and is compelled to touch it, it is revealed that this 'perfect' plant is in fact made of metal!

Leading from the South Lawn into the walled garden is another gateway, simpler but nevertheless impressive in its scale and guarded by two all-seeing eagles. Disappointingly, this is today almost entirely grassed over, with a tennis court at one end marring the view through the gateway. On the

This splendid Aloe is actually made of metal.

north wall however is a reminder of times past – an old greenhouse still stands and is used to store garden tools, although many of its panes are broken, its wooden frame sun-bleached and shaky, and its stone base chipped. It is the tiled roof of this structure that hints at its significance. The glass roofs that we take for granted in a greenhouse were actually only used from the nineteenth century onwards, so the tiles on this one demonstrate a rare survival of the earlier style. An Ordnance Survey map of 1875 shows that this was once only one of many greenhouses at Dorfold,[13] and I hope that this structure, whose humble appearance belies its significance as an artefact, is not allowed to collapse entirely. Unfortunately, a second walled garden is in an even sadder state, being filled with Christmas trees.

The same map shows a walk between two flower borders that stretched below the south boundary of the walled garden. Having once been lost, this garden has been reinstated in recent years, and is again a pleasant corner of Dorfold.[14] Romantic plants such as phlox and salvias flower on either side of a grass path,

sheltered by the tall red brick wall, with a pretty but simple iron gate at one end and a wooden arbour at the other. Stretching right round this area and the two walled gardens was, in the nineteenth century at least, a walk, which must have enjoyed pleasant views of the park.[15]

To the eastern side of the South Lawn, steps lead down to a sun-dappled woodland garden which was planted in the 1980s. Hidden in a dell in the midst of this is a delightful water garden, which has been developed from a rockery which is dated at the beginning of the twentieth century from the '1908' carved on the steps leading to it. In fact, the water in this garden reflects the fact that this area was once the tip of a pool that began near the front drive, as is shown in the 1875 Ordnance Survey map.[16] Here, mossy stones frame twisting paths and a gurgling stream edged with foxgloves and astilbes passes down naturalistic rills to form a pool, planted with lilies. This is a tranquil area which is not overly-maintained, to create a 'secret' corner of the gardens. The paths are overgrown in places and the azaleas are dotted with

A statue of Shakespeare marks the date of Dorfold's construction.

leaves from the tree canopy above, left to rest where they have fallen, just as the rest of the Dorfold gardens have been left, in many ways, to find their own 'comfort zone'.

Above: Smart gates lead into the walled garden.
Below: A gateway is re-used from a demolished Nantwich building.

Above: Dorfold is home to an important surviving early greenhouse.
Below: Astilbes, hostas & lilies crowd into the woodland garden.

Select Bibliography

'Dorfold Hall, Cheshire: The Seat of Mr Henry J. Tollemache'. *Country Life*, 31ˢᵗ October 1908, p594-606.
Dorfold Hall, Nantwich, Cheshire, (Guide Leaflet).
English Heritage Register of Parks and Gardens of Special Historic Interest, 1999.
Hall, SC. *The Baronial Halls, Picturesque Edifices, and Ancient Churches of England*. Chapman and Hall, London, 1848.
Laurie, Ian. 'Nesfield in Cheshire'. *Garden History*, Volume 15, Number 2, 1987, p145-155.
Ordnance Survey 25" to 1 mile, Cheshire Sheet 55.16, 1st edition 1875.

The archive material used is held at the John Rylands Library (Roundell Muniments).

References

1. Ian Laurie. 'Nesfield in Cheshire'. *Garden History*, Volume 15, Number 2, 1987, p148.
2. Roundell Muniments, I Deeds and Allied Documents, Chester, Dorfold, Wilbraham Spencer Tollemache.
3. Roundell Muniments, I Deeds and Allied Documents, Chester, Dorfold, Wilbraham Spencer Tollemache.
4. Roundell Muniments, I Deeds and Allied Documents, Chester, Dorfold, Wilbraham Spencer Tollemache.
5. Roundell Muniments, I Deeds and Allied Documents, Chester, Dorfold, Wilbraham Spencer Tollemache.
6. SC Hall. *The Baronial Halls, Picturesque Edifices, and Ancient Churches of England*. Chapman and Hall, London, 1848.
7. *English Heritage Register of Parks and Gardens of Special Historic Interest*, 1999.
8. 'Dorfold Hall, Cheshire: The Seat of Mr Henry J. Tollemache'. *Country Life*, 31ˢᵗ October 1908, p595.
9. 'Dorfold Hall, Cheshire: The Seat of Mr Henry J. Tollemache'. *Country Life*, 31ˢᵗ October 1908, p596.
10. 'Dorfold Hall, Cheshire: The Seat of Mr Henry J. Tollemache'. *Country Life*, 31ˢᵗ October 1908, p601.
11. *Dorfold Hall, Nantwich, Cheshire*, (guide leaflet).
12. 'Dorfold Hall, Cheshire: The Seat of Mr Henry J. Tollemache'. *Country Life*, 31ˢᵗ October 1908, p600.
13. *Ordnance Survey 25" to 1 mile*, Cheshire Sheet 55.16, 1st edition 1875.
14. *Ordnance Survey 25" to 1 mile*, Cheshire Sheet 55.16, 1st edition 1875.
15. *Ordnance Survey 25" to 1 mile*, Cheshire Sheet 55.16, 1st edition 1875.
16. *Ordnance Survey 25" to 1 mile*, Cheshire Sheet 55.16, 1st edition 1875.

Rode Hall, Scholar Green

O ver the past century it has become an assumption that historic houses must struggle to maintain their viability in the modern world in order to survive. The most common outcomes of this battle seem to be acquisition by the National Trust or some other heritage organisation; conversion for a multi-occupancy residence; use as a hotel or conference venue; dereliction; or demolition in order for the land to be used for new developments. The latter fate was suffered by the once thriving Thelwall Hall, near Lymm, prompting a long-time local resident, Miss Joan Williamson, to rue the day that 'the wretched builder came along – he demolished everything'. Such passion is because these big houses do not stand entirely alone as elite enclaves of the wealthy. Instead, they act as landmarks and create local character and community, with Thelwall Hall holding wonderful parties for the nearby residents. For this reason, historic houses leave an emotional as well as a physical gap when they are lost. Rode Hall, near Alsager, is of a comparable size to that at Thelwall and so it is a real pleasure to find that it has enjoyed far better fortunes, being still privately-owned as a family home and, even more of a rarity, a home to the same family as when it was first built in the eighteenth century. What is more, its current owner, Sir Richard Baker Wilbraham, regularly opens the house and gardens to the public, with the many return-visitors proving that Rode Hall still holds the interest of the community.

The Hall was bought from the Rode family by Roger Wilbraham of Nantwich in 1669,[1] and then rebuilt by his son Randle at the very beginning of the eighteenth century. This building was then greatly enlarged by Randle II who in 1752 added a new block, converting the old brick hall into a service range. In

Top: Beautifully clear water trickles from the 'Stews' to the Rode lake. Inset: A modern Wood Nymph sculpture has replaced a Victorian urn in the Nesfield garden.

The Rode lake, known as 'Rode Pool', is the focus of the view from the house.

Rode's grotto is one of many that were popular in the 18th-century, designed to look almost like natural caves.

The brick tunnel boathouse

Rode's walled garden has recently been restored & is now in good working order.

The 'old' Rode Hall, which was joined by a new block in the late-18th-century.

the early nineteenth century architects John Hope and then Lewis Wyatt worked on Rode, with the old and new houses being linked. Today this makes quite a sizeable frontage, especially with the adjoining stable block, thought also to be of Randle II's time.[2]

Randle II exerted his influence not only on the house at Rode, but also on its setting, creating the gothic eyecatcher that sits dramatically on a nearby hill at Mow Cop, now owned by the National Trust. With the dramatic look of a ruined grey stone castle on a rocky outcrop, this folly certainly provides an interesting feature on the horizon but in fact, according to Sir Richard, it was built as a summerhouse to be the venue for family picnics, presumably because of its absolutely stunning views over Cheshire. Such eyecatchers were popular in the eighteenth century, when it was considered an aspect of garden design to draw attention to the wider landscape, with an interesting built feature on the horizon being the perfect way to do this. A famous eighteenth century eyecatcher is the round, battlemented Folly Tower at Tabley Hall, near Knutsford, the view of which across Tabley Mere was painted by artist JMW Turner during his stays there in 1808.

Mary Bootle, the wife of Randle II's son Richard Wilbraham Bootle (who took the name 'Bootle' as a stipulation of his uncle Sir Thomas Bootle's will) is responsible for one of the two attributes to win the Rode landscape a serious place in garden history, commissioning Humphry Repton to draw up a Red Book in 1790. In fact, Repton never actually carried out his plans, but the next occupier, Randle III, did bring in John Webb to undertake the work. The Red Book is therefore well worth some attention. When Repton visited Rode, the parkland was in agricultural use, prompting him to write that: 'The landscape in its present state is not unpleasing considered merely as a landscape; but it is much more consistent with the view from a Cottage or farm house than from the Portico of a Gentleman's Seat'.[3] To give Rode's setting a more appropriate tone, he suggested flooding a lake, and making various changes to the hall approaches. When Webb came to Rode a decade later, existing pools were extended to create a lake with the work, Sir Richard speculates, perhaps being carried out by Napoleonic prisoners of war. This lake, known as Rode Pool, forms the focus of the view from the house even today, although the line of sight is often more obscured by undergrowth than Repton or Webb would have liked. The current generations of Wilbrahams use a small wooden boathouse for ventures onto the water, but keep on show an older brick tunnel boathouse, which looks almost like a natural feature as it sits at the end of a quiet inlet, its roof covered in grass.

The walk to the lake from the house is very pleasant, passing by this inlet and also a woodland pool known as 'the Stews' ('stew' being a term used to describe a pond in which fish for

Top: The late-18th-century 'new' hall makes a sizeable frontage with the adjoining 'old' hall & stable block. Bottom: Nearby Mow Cop was built as an eyecatcher for Rode Hall.

the kitchen were kept). It is thought that this area was originally landscaped by John Webb,[4] but it has recently been improved to create a tranquil spot in which bamboos, gunnera and pink astilbes are reflected in the beautifully clear water, which trickles down a stone restraining wall and then towards the lake.

Beyond the Stews, and thought to have been ornamented at around the same time, is an area known as the Wild Garden. Here, specimen trees and rhododendrons crowd around a quiet grassy spot at the bottom of a substantial pit, perhaps originally dug out in order to make bricks for building work at Rode. Nestling here is a small pool where the stream that feeds the Stews rises. This water was once used to supply the house and, according to Sir Richard, recent tests showed it to still be healthier than the current supply of tap water! To one side of this glade is a large rockery, in which twisting stone steps and paths through walls of boulders lead amongst trees and shrubs. Here, amongst foxgloves and ferns and marked with

a rough stone cross, lurks a rustic grotto, unfortunately in some disrepair, which is carved out from a hillock and is still lined in places with decorative shells. Such grottos had become very popular in England in the eighteenth century and although often manmade, they were designed to look almost like natural caves, encouraging the visitor's imagination to run wild.

The landscape park has regressed to being largely in agricultural use once more. As a result, it is criss-crossed with fences for grazing sheep and in places planted with crops, such as maize, although it is hoped that it may be possible to restore it to its ornamental appearance in time. One interesting relic in the park is an eighteenth-century ice-house, sitting within sight of the front of the hall. This would have been used in the days long before fridges to store ice from the lake for keeping food cool and for making ice-cream, amongst other things – a prestigious asset to any house. In the 1980s a great deal of work was done on this oncecrumbling structure when a local bricklayer

Although the brick boathouse still exists, the Wilbraham family now use a simple wooden one for trips onto the lake.

passes a herbaceous border planted recently by the current Lady Baker Wilbraham, to look over the steep drop down to the Wild Garden. From the house, two grass terraces and stone steps marked with urns descend to a yew-hedged rose garden. This is largely grass now, but the clipped golden yews remain and in-dentations of the original flowerbeds can still be made out and the main, ring-shaped bed is still present, although Lady Baker Wilbraham has planted it mainly with herbaceous plants as roses did not do well there. Even this 'sur-viving' Nesfield scheme is not exactly as he intended it: as well as many of the flowerbeds having been hidden under grass, Sir Richard's parents altered the central design, removing the climbing rose ropes, and adding a star-shaped bed in the centre. This is essentially the garden

confessed that his lifelong ambition had been to repair such a thing. It is now slightly differ-ent from its original state as the entrance was made straight from the intended 'L' shape which used to keep out drafts. It is well worth a small detour from the gardens, not least because of the almost psychedelic effect of staring down into its thirty foot deep brick-lined interior.

The next notable stage of landscape devel-opment at Rode took place under Randle IV, who in 1861 brought William Andrews Nesfield to work on the gardens nearer the house. Nesfield was prolific in Cheshire and a Nesfield-designed approach still exists at Dorfold, but most of his formal garden designs have been lost to wartime crop-growing, re-source cutbacks, and changes in fashion. We are fortunate however that at Rode the terraced gardens do remain, to a great degree still match-ing the Nesfield plan which is held in the house.[5]

A colonnaded doorway leads from the house to a gravelled terrace walk which at one end

we see today, although another change took place in 1989. The Victorian urn in the centre of this arrangement was broken during the storms of that year and so was replaced with a sculpture of a wood nymph by David Williams Ellis.

More of Nesfield's arrangement exists to the north of here, where there is a simple lime avenue. At one end of this is a rustic red brick and wooden summerhouse thought to date

Top, middle & bottom: A David Williams Ellis Wood Nymph sculpture now stands in the middle of the W A Nesfield garden, one of the very few to survive in Cheshire.

Opposite page: The grotto is framed by lush ferns & hostas.

from the time of Nesfield's involvement, and at the other is another ring, this time gravelled, the island of which contains three beeches. These splendid trees are of mature years which gives them gravitas but causes Sir Richard some sleepless nights as he worries about them falling down.

One of Rode's special draws is its kitchen garden which has not only been restored, with work having been done on the walls and glasshouses, but has been returned to genuine working use with its produce feeding not only the main household, but also being sold (by the gardener's mother on the A50!). The sight of row upon row of unapologetic onions, cabbages, cutting flowers, and enormous prizewinning gooseberries grown by Head Gardener Kelvin Archer is certainly refreshing in an age when kitchen gardens are often either derelict or 'restored' to sport only a few ornamental vegetables amongst more decorative planting. Here it is clear that a kitchen garden can be pretty without sacrificing any of its productivity. The pear growing over the wooden door to the garden, the clay cloches left amongst the artichokes by the brick shed, and the idyllic rose-covered Gardener's Cottage, which is lived in by Kelvin Archer, all demonstrate that often it is evidence of real life that bring an authenticity to a garden. Alongside the outer wall of the kitchen garden, Lady Baker Wilbraham is developing a pretty laburnum walk, where once was the 'Colonel's Walk', leading to 'Ladies' Walk', which was used by the family in the nineteenth century to access the church along a private route.[6]

Rode is today open to the public and Sir Richard has so far successfully trodden the fine line of attracting paying visitors, without there being so many, and so many compromises made for them, that it loses the appealing atmosphere of a private family home. So far, Rode Hall seems to have thrived on its sideline as a tourist attraction and, as Sir Richard says, having the public in the garden is a great incentive for keeping it tidy. I cannot imagine how his wife, who works with the gardeners, feels about this however!

The kitchen garden produces all kinds of fruit & vegetables, including artichokes, pears & cutting flowers.

The Gardener's Cottage has an idyllic setting, surrounded by cutting flowers.

Select Bibliography

Aslet, Clive. 'Rode Hall, Cheshire: The Seat of Sir Richard Baker Wilbraham'. *Country Life*, 2nd May 1985, p1186-1191.
English Heritage Register of Parks and Gardens of Special Historic Interest, 1999.
Laurie, Ian. 'Nesfield in Cheshire'. *Garden History*, Volume 15, Number 2, 1987, p145-155.
Rode Hall and Gardens. Jarrold Publishing, Norwich, 1998.
Stead, Bob. 'Sir Richard Baker Wilbraham'. *Cheshire Life*, May 1991, p46-49.

The archive material used is held at Rode Hall and in the Cheshire Record Office (Baker Wilbraham Family of Odd Rode).

References

1   *Rode Hall and Gardens*. 1998, p2.
2   *English Heritage Register of Parks and Gardens of Special Historic Interest*, 1999.
3   Humphry Repton. *Red Book for Rode Hall*. 1790.
4   *English Heritage Register of Parks and Gardens of Special Historic Interest*, 1999.
5   WA Nesfield. 'Plan of proposed works at Rode Hall'. 1861.
6   *Rode Hall and Gardens*. 1998, p14.

Birkenhead Park, the Wirral

$\mathcal{F}$or much of Britain's history designed open space for recreational use had, to a large extent, been the prerogative of the wealthy but in the nineteenth century this had to change as the population balance shifted so that ever increasing numbers were living in the towns and cities. As we appreciate today, the kind of high density urban living that sprang up can bring its own brand of social problems and the Victorians became particularly concerned about public health and well-being. In 1833 a report was drawn up by a Select Committee on Public Walks to 'consider the best means of securing Open Spaces in the Vicinity of populous Towns, as Public Walks and Places of Exercise, calculated to promote the Health and Comfort of the Inhabitants'.[1] This drew attention to the lack of open public space in urban areas, and the detrimental effect this would have on the general populace, and in particular on those it refers to as 'the humbler classes': 'little or no provision has been made for Public Walks or Open Spaces, fitted to afford means of exercise or amusement to the middle or humbler classes'.[2] The response was a proliferation of public parks, funded by donations from wealthy individuals, public subscription, or town councils. In this mood the public park was born, as a way of giving the people a place to enjoy fresh air, undertake physical exercise, appreciate nature, pass the time other than in the taverns and, conveniently, also a place for different social groups to mingle, thus reducing any potential class tension.[3] Most of these parks we can still enjoy today, although many have sadly declined due to funding cuts in recent decades, threatening the return of all those problems the Victorians hoped to cure.

Birkenhead Park is one of the most famous parks to be established in the wake of the Select

*Top: The Swiss Bridge was one of several interesting
structures to decorate Birkenhead Park.*

Aerial plan of Birkenhead Park
(Mike Garbutt, Wirral Metropolitan
Borough Council Parks and Open Spaces).

*Although restored in the 1980s, the Boathouse viewing platform
& bandstand quickly fell into disrepair again.*

Committee report, which in fact referred specifically to the flood of people who headed to the Wirral because of the lack of open space across the Mersey. Liverpool resident John Ashton Yates gave evidence that: 'In consequence of the want of open walks and fresh air, and the difficulty of getting to them, there is a large population now rising up on the other side of the river, in the county of Cheshire, to which the people resort in multitudes, particularly on the Sunday to the great annoyance of many good people who reside on that side.'[4] As Yates suggested, Birkenhead in the nineteenth century was something of a boomtown. Its position on the Wirral peninsula gives it a slightly detached air but it nevertheless had easy links with Liverpool, encouraging commuters to set up home in Birkenhead, whose consequent growth then lead to the development of shipyards and other industries. By 1842 the town's astonishing population increase had prompted the Birkenhead Improvement Commission to raise funds in order to create a public park. To get the project underway, the individual members of the Commission bought the land out of their own pockets, and then sold it to the town once it had secured funding.[5] As with Regent's Park in London, the longer-term plan was to create smart houses around the park which would benefit from its facilities and in turn raise money for the project from their sale.

To design the park the Commission recruited designer Joseph Paxton, who had already worked at Tatton Park as well as being Head Gardener at Chatsworth. Edward Kemp, who had worked under Paxton at Chatsworth was then brought on board to oversee the work as Park Superintendent and stayed until his death in 1891.

It was clear that a public park such as this would demand a new type of design as the principles previously used for landscape parks and private gardens were not appropriate to this entirely different role. Paxton rose to the challenge and introduced an ingenious system of traffic circulation, meandering walks, earth

sculpting and clever planting in order to create the illusion of privacy, space and surprise that would bring a little bit of nature's work to the urban populace, albeit in a refined format.

Birkenhead Park is designed in two parts, Upper and Lower Parks, which are divided by a road designed to enable traffic to pass through so that the park does not act as a huge obstacle in the centre of town. Each part is however entirely complementary, being designed in tandem, and it is easy to cross the road from one to the other. The focus of each is an artificial lake, which is a useful way of tackling what is a rather marshy, clay site. Both lakes are modest in size, but this is concealed by their sinuous and undulating banks and also the carefully placed islands – the visitor's hope of getting a clear view is refused from all angles and instead he imagines the great expanses of lake that lie beyond his view. In the nineteenth century the lakes were filled with goldfish, aquatic plants and swans – today people still use the lake for fishing, and the odd bird can be seen, but the effect is rather less ornamental.[6] To add to the impression of infinite size, the walks around them cut through deep 'ravines' in mounds which were created with the waste from the lakes. These mounds are scattered with dramatic boulders, which were once planted with mosses and rock-plants, and are covered with trees, which were originally underplanted with ferns and shrubs.[7] Edward Kemp became a great proponent of these kinds of twisting paths, writing in *How to Lay Out a Small Garden*: 'Variety may be partly obtained in gardens by serpentine walks … a serpentine walk, in which several of the curves are seen at once, or where they very much resemble each other in sweep, loses the chief and most engaging part of its variety. It is of prime concern, therefore, that the curves in a walk should be as varied as much as they can be in their length and expansion, and that they should not be exposed to each other at any point'.[8] In Birkenhead at its most civilised, the experience is of a stroll in the forest, and at its least civilised it feels like a science fiction adventure because today there are problems with the extensive drainage system so the paths become blocked with leaves and flood causing the walk to become rather too exciting, both physically and visually.

Adding interest and even mystery are the islands and built features that embellish the views. The lake in the Lower Park contains an irregular and wooded island, leading to which is a decorative Swiss Bridge, with ornate panelling and a tiled roof supported by simple pillars. Paxton originally had five other bridges leading to this island[9] but these were demolished in the 1970s. Watching over this lake from a raised promontory on the western shore is a pavilion that was intended to be used as a bandstand, under which is a boathouse. Having fallen into disrepair with the rest of the park, this fantastic little building was restored using funds from Mobil Oil in the 1980s, but sadly is already in a bad state again, the work having been carried out with a naivety that did not appreciate the importance of using specific building techniques when restoring old build-

ings. Standing here, one can fondly imagine the pleasure (perhaps looking through rose-tinted spectacles) that this view must have given the people of Birkenhead. Today, you are likely to be sharing it with the local youth and their cans of beer, but this is perhaps a testament to the draw that the park still has as a place to while away the leisure hours.

The lakes and their planted walks occupy a deceptively small area of the park, and around them are great open grassed areas, intersected with paths. These would originally have been planted with clumps of exotic trees.[10] Forming a ring around the edge is Park Drive, which was intended for carriages and can still be toured by cars at a leisurely pace, allowing drivers and cyclists to use and enjoy the park without spoiling the perambulation of pedestrians. This drive and the other walks were laid with macadam, compressed layers of broken stones, in this case 'Red Jersey Gravel'.[11]

Park Drive offers an excellent way to admire the villas that border the park. These are the houses that were so central to the original

Birkenhead Park is well-used by Canada geese as well as local people.

plans, although not as many of them were built as had been hoped. The houses that stand to-day are beautiful buildings but are clearly not kept as the smart family residences they were intended to be; rather, many are used as offices or are in a state of disrepair.

Also serving as reminders to the grand intentions for Birkenhead Park are the six lodges one at each of its entrances, largely the responsibility of John Robertson, Paxton's architectural assistant. Between them they offer a spectrum of styles: the Gothic Lodge, Italian Lodge, Castellated Lodge, the East and West Norman Lodges (actually Greek Revival in style), and Central Lodge (Italianate). The most spectacular is the Grand Entrance Gateway which towers high above the streets outside, trumpeting the park's great import. It has three huge arches framed with pillars, a wide central one for carriages, and two smaller ones for pedestrians. It is so large as to have rooms not only in the lodges on either side, but even above the arches. Such a gateway would seem a trifle presumptuous even in Rome but in this setting

it just blows the visitor away being, I hope the people of Birkenhead will forgive me for saying, spectacularly out of place on the residential streets. Indeed, even Paxton did not entirely approve of the size of this lodge, the designer of which was Lewis Hornblower, a Liverpool architect who later also worked at Sefton Park across the Mersey.[12]

Not all of Paxton's design was spot-on straightaway. There was initially no provision for sporting activities because such things had yet to become popular – unthinkable in this day and age. It soon became clear though that such provision was necessary, and some of the open meadows in Paxton's design were converted to cricket pitches. By the 1880s it was recognised that physical exercise was an important and enjoyable form of recreation and that providing for this was a useful way to at-

tract people to parks. Stamford Park in Altrincham claims to be the first public park in Britain to be designed with sporting provision already made.[13]

In the early days, the park was a source of great pride for the town. Having visited in the early 1850s, the American Frederick Law Olmsted wrote: 'The baker had begged us not

Top: Designer Joseph Paxton created earth mounds & piled them with rocks to create a sense of drama.
Middle: Paxton established large open meadows, which still remain today.
Bottom: The lakes appear bigger than they really are.

to leave Birkenhead without seeing their new park.'[14] He concludes that the people's pride in the park is because of the sense of ownership they had: 'And all this magnificent pleasure-ground is entirely, unreservedly, and for ever the people's own. The poorest British peasant is as free to enjoy it in all its parts as the British queen. More than that, the baker of Birkenhead has the pride of an owner in it'.[15]

Olmsted's description of the park is invaluable for giving a sense of its heyday: 'I will only tell you, that we passed by winding paths, over acres and acres, with a constant varying surface, where on all sides were growing every variety of shrubs and flowers, with more than natural grace, all set in borders of greenest, closest turf, and all kept with most consummate neatness. At a distance of a quarter of a mile

der which a flock of sheep were reposing, and girls and women with children, were playing. While watching the cricketeers, we were threatened with a shower, and hastened back to look for shelter, which we found in a pagoda, on an island approached by a Chinese bridge. It was soon filled, as were the other ornamental buildings, by a crowd of those who, like ourselves, had been overtaken in the grounds by the rain; and I was glad to observe that the privileges of the garden were enjoyed about equally by all classes. There were some who were attended by servants, and sent at once for their carriages, but a large proportion were of the common ranks, and a few women with children, or suffering from ill-health, were evidently the wives of very humble labourers.'[16]

Olmsted was himself extremely impressed

from the gate, we came to an open field of clean, bright, green-sward, closely mown, on which a large tent was pitched, and a party of boys in one part, and a party of gentlemen in another, were playing cricket. Beyond this was a large meadow with rich groups of trees, un-

by the park, the like of which had not yet been seen in America: 'Five minutes of admiration, and a few more spent in studying the manner in which art had been employed to obtain from nature so much beauty, and I was ready to admit that in democratic America there was noth-

Above: A walk in Birkenhead Park can feel like a forest adventure.

ing to be thought of as comparable with this People's Garden. Indeed, gardening, had here reached a perfection that I had never dreamed of. I cannot undertake to describe the effect of so much taste and skill as had evidently been employed'.[17] Olmsted was no innocent American tourist though, rather he was already working as a landscape architect and, inspired by his visit to Birkenhead went on to design Central Park in New York, which uses many of the same design 'tricks' as its English cousin, copying in particular its manipulation of traffic with a cut-through road and circuitous drive.

In spite of its American connection however, Birkenhead Park's importance has too often been overlooked and during the twentieth century it fell into decline. This was due to the usual trap of poor funding and maintenance afflicted on the United Kingdom's public parks as a result of cost cutting and misguided man-

agement at governmental and local authority level. Now however, Mike Garbutt, the council officer responsible for Birkenhead Park (Wirral Metropolitan Borough Council Parks and Open Spaces Project Officer), is delighted that it has secured millions of pounds funding from the Heritage Lottery Fund, the European Regional Development Fund and Wirral Waterfront to restore it to the condition so admired by Olmsted. Work will take place over five years so as not to cause too much disruption to the public and will include restoration of the paths, drainage, lodges, and Swiss Bridge. In order to ensure that it then stays in good condition, maintenance will now be ongoing, and security guards employed to look after the welfare of both the park and its users. Birkenhead Park is one of the country's most significant and influential landscapes – hopefully it will now be treated as such!

The Grand Entrance Gateway made a bold statement in the park's heyday,
but now looks rather out-of-place on Birkenhead's streets.
(Mike Garbutt, Wirral Metropolitan Borough Council Parks and Open Spaces)

Select Bibliography

Colquhoun, Kate. *A Thing in Disguise: The Visionary Life of Joseph Paxton*. Fourth Estate, London, 2003.

Colquhoun, Kate. 'The Man who gave Parks to the People'. *Country Life*, 12ᵗʰ June 2003, p112-113.

Conway, Hazel. *Public Parks*. Shire Publications, Buckinghamshire, 1996.

English Heritage Register of Parks and Gardens of Special Historic Interest, 1999.

Irish University Press Series of British Parliamentary Papers: Reports from Select Committees on Public Walks and on the Improvement of the Metropolis with Minutes of Evidence Appendices and Index. Urban Areas Planning 1, Shannon, Ireland, 1968.

Jordan, Harriet. 'Public Parks, 1885-1914'. *Garden History*, Volume 22, Number 1, 1994, p85-113.

Kemp, Edward. *How to Lay Out a Small Garden*. Bradbury and Evans, London, 1850.

Olmsted, Frederick. *Walks and Talks of an American Farmer in England*. George P Putnam, New York, 1852.

Shoemaker, Candice, ed. *Encyclopedia of Gardens: History and Design*. Fitzroy Dearborn, London, 2001.

Tate, Alan. *Great City Parks*, Spon Press, London, 2001.

Taylor, Hilary. 'Urban Public Parks, 1840-1900: Design and Meaning'. *Garden History*, Volume 23, Number 2, 1995, p201-221.

References

1   *Irish University Press Series of British Parliamentary Papers: Reports from Select Committees on Public Walks and on the Improvement of the Metropolis with Minutes of Evidence Appendices and Index. Urban Areas Planning 1*, 1968, p3.

2   *Irish University Press Series of British Parliamentary Papers: Reports from Select Committees on Public Walks and on the Improvement of the Metropolis with Minutes of Evidence Appendices and Index. Urban Areas Planning 1*, 1968, p3.

3   Hazel Conway. *Public Parks*. 1996, p5.

4   *Irish University Press Series of British Parliamentary Papers: Reports from Select Committees on Public Walks and on the Improvement of the Metropolis with Minutes of Evidence Appendices and Index. Urban Areas Planning 1*, 1968, p42.

5   Kate Colquhoun. *A Thing in Disguise: The Visionary Life of Joseph Paxton*. 2003, p120.

6   Frederick Olmsted. *Walks and Talks of an American Farmer in England*. 1852, p80.

7   Frederick Olmsted. *Walks and Talks of an American Farmer in England*. 1852, p81.

8   Edward Kemp. *How to Lay Out a Small Garden*. 1850, p61.

9   Candice Shoemaker, ed. *Encyclopedia of Gardens: History and Design*. 2001, p144.

10 Alan Tate. *Great City Parks*. 2001, p81.

11 Alan Tate. *Great City Parks*. 2001, p81.

12 Kate Colquhoun. *A Thing in Disguise: The Visionary Life of Joseph Paxton*. 2003, p135.

13 Harriet Jordan. 'Public Parks, 1885-1914'. *Garden History*, Volume 22, Number 1, 1994, p86.

14 Frederick Olmsted. *Walks and Talks of an American Farmer in England*. 1852, p78.

15 Frederick Olmsted. *Walks and Talks of an American Farmer in England*. 1852, p80.

16 Frederick Olmsted. *Walks and Talks of an American Farmer in England*. 1852, p78.

17 Frederick Olmsted. *Walks and Talks of an American Farmer in England*. 1852, p78.

Grosvenor Park, Chester

E dward Kemp worked as Parks Superintendent of Birkenhead Park for almost half a century but this did not occupy his time so much that he was not able to undertake other projects. When the 2nd Marquess of Westminster decided in 1867 to donate a public park to the city of Chester, where he owned a great deal of the land, Kemp was given the commission of designing it. Much like the reasons behind that at Birkenhead, Grosvenor Park, which was named after its benefactor, was created from a spirit of improving the situation of the common urban man. The Marquess wrote that his intention in donating the park to the town was 'as a gift on my part to the Citizens of Chester hoping it may afford health and recreation to themselves and their Families for many years to come'.[1]

The Marquess was particular about the nature of this recreation though; music such as band concerts was to be allowed, but dancing was certainly not. The 1868 bye-laws include the stipulation that: 'No Fairs, Political or other Public Meetings nor open air preaching shall be held in any part of the Park neither shall the Park or any part thereof be used for dancing or for the celebration of the Anniversaries or other re-unions of Clubs or Benefit Societies.'[2] Other laws asserted that: 'Every person who shall climb any Tree pluck or gather any Flower Fruit or Berry of any description whatsover shall for every offence forfeit and pay a Sum not exceeding Forty shillings', that a similar fine was payable by any person found playing 'Football Cricket or any other Game', or indeed any person 'who shall play upon or sound any musical instrument without the permission of the Council'.[3] The Marquess also endowed the park with £100 per year to help pay for its maintenance.[4]

Grosvenor Park opened in the same year and has continued to be admired ever since. Endurance in a park is usually a sign of things having been 'got right' at the design stage and Kemp was certainly a great believer in the importance of good design, writing in the preface to *How to Lay Out a Small Garden* that: 'There is a humanising and elevating influence about everything that is really beautiful, whether in Art or Nature, that it is almost impossible for the observant wayfarer to stumble up on such objects without being cheered and benefited; while their effect on those who have them daily beneath their eye is of a still deeper kind.'[5]

Grosvenor Park's benefactor, the Marquess of Westminster,
is depicted in white marble.

*Norman ruins add a tone
of tranquility.*

*The park perches high
above the River Dee.*

Grosvenor Park enjoys bright flowerbeds & fine trees.

The park's great distinguishing feature is a pair of holly & lime avenues.

Grosvenor Park's main boon is the position it holds on a terrace overlooking the river Dee from the north bank, giving it something like the feel of a European town park. To the east of the park is St John's Church and its accompanying Norman ruins, and as these are visible and accessible, they add a tone of antiquity. There is plenty of interest within the park though, without having to look out to the view. The main Union Street entrance in the north was designed by the busy Chester architect John Douglas, who also worked at the Marquess' home at Eaton Hall, and has wrought-iron carriage gates with matching gates on each side for pedestrians. Here is a pretty black and white lodge decorated with wooden figures of William the Conqueror and the Norman Earls of Chester. From this entrance an avenue walk reaches through the park towards the river and this is lined with alternate clipped limes and huge hollies forming the park's most distinctive feature. Before it reaches the river, the walk meets another similar avenue which stretches from east to west and is broken with quatre-foil flowerbeds planted with bright colours and ending with an ornamental gateway leading to St John's. The meeting of these two walks is acknowledged with a square flowerbed, which is edged in stone and today planted with cheerful annuals. Standing boldly in the bed is a knightly representation of the park's benefactor, reproduced in white marble by Thomas Thornycroft in 1869, a few years after the park originally opened. On the plinth of this, the Marquess is described as 'The Generous Land-lord, The Friend of the Distressed, The Helper of all Good Works, The Benefactor to this City'. He is in fact represented so large as to be best admired from a short distance away, where there is a raised terrace. The low walls of this include a curved stone bench, which faces the Marquess, although by turning round we can enjoy the lovely view across the river to cows grazing in a meadow, although this is often rather obscured by tree growth. Tucked into the wall below is an ornamental octagonal pump house, designed by John Douglas, which is known as Billy Hobby's Well.

A walk in the west of the park gives more of a feeling of adventure, twisting through a rocky grassed nook and through a corner oozing with the feeling of delicious antiquity, where the visitor passes amongst and under various gothic and medieval arches brought to the park from other locations in Chester. In the eastern part are lawns decorated with flowerbeds boasting gay bedding schemes. These are very popular but do not feature in the original planting plan for 'Chester Park', which is held in the Cheshire Record Office. This instead emphasises shrubs and specimen trees, including *Pinus excelsa*, Weeping mountain ash, *Wellingtonia japonica*, red-flowering horse chestnuts, purple beeches, red dogwoods, hybrid rhododendrons and many hollies, such as yellow-berried holly, variegated prickly holly, and Hodgins' holly.[6] There are also post-1867 additions: a 1950s hillside rockery, giant Californian redwood trees (*Sequoia Sempervirens*), Arts and Crafts shelters, a miniature railway, an early twentieth-century sunken pond and rose planted stone terraces.

Today the park is in excellent condition compared to many suffering urban parks, but it has experienced mixed fortunes during its lifetime. Its official opening in 1867 was marked with a celebration, which the Marquess was unfortunately unable to attend, organised by a special council committee. Festivities included a special dinner at the Grosvenor Hotel, as recorded in Council Minutes: 'the Committee had seen the Manager of the Grosvenor Hotel, who had undertaken to provide a first class Dejeuner including Soup and a choice dessert at the prices fixed by the Committee.'[7] During the day, a procession including the Cheshire Volunteer Fire Brigade and the Wax and Tallow Chandlers' Company accompanied the mayor and town council to the park, and a special poem was even written by local poet J. Housden:

'Hail to the grand eventful day,
And may its lustre shine
Upon the donor I do pray,
With glories all sublime.

He is a worthy gen'rous friend,
A nobleman so grand,
Whose love and kindness does extend
Throughout our native land.

We hail the Marquess with delight,
We thank him for his deed;
The park is a delightful sight,
A princely gift indeed.

My noble Lord and Marchioness,
The park we do admire;
Our gratitude we all express,
No more do ye require.

For wealth they have, and splendour too,
I trust a peaceful mind;
They study what is best to do,
To benefit mankind.

May love and peace, and grace defend
The noble happy pair,
And may their lives for years extend,
Which is my fervent prayer.

May happiness and grace abound,
And virtue still increase,
Until they hear the joyful sound
In realms of joy and peace.'[8]

Grosvenor Park was not always so fortunate though. Writing in *Cheshire Life* in 1944, C. Aylott Martyn commented that: '"Digging for Victory" has meant that the flower beds are now mainly planted with foodstuffs of various descriptions'.[9] The days of growing vegetables in the park are long gone, but in recent memory it has been rather threatened by the nature of its main users, who tend to be drug-users and skateboarding teenagers, whose boards can cause a surprising amount of damage. On a recent visit however, I was treated to a cup of tea by a gentleman whose enthusiasm for visiting the park earned him a job patrolling it for security. He feeds the ducks, but rather more seriously keeps an eye out for used needles, and claims to have found eighty-three in one week when he first started, but now, hearteningly, this is down to only a couple. This surely is real evidence that parks need people in order to work. In recent decades it has been thought possible to leave them to their own devices but the fact is that they were designed to be a joint effort between nature and man, with man being a park keeper, and this is still what is needed for their success.

Select Bibliography

Conway, Hazel. *Public Parks*. Shire Publications, Buckinghamshire, 1996.
English Heritage Register of Parks and Gardens of Special Historic Interest, 2001.
Kemp, Edward. *How to Lay Out a Small Garden*. Bradbury and Evans, London, 1850.
Martyn, C. Aylott. 'Some Historic Chester Gardens'. *Cheshire Life*, Volume 10, Number 9, March 1944, p8-11.

The archive material used is held in the Cheshire Record Office.

References

1   Cheshire Record Office Z/CB/2 9th October 1867.
2   Cheshire Record Office CCF/3Part 13 Grosvenor Park Bye-laws of 12/2/1868.
3   Cheshire Record Office CCF/3Part 13 Grosvenor Park Bye-laws of 12/2/1868.
4   Cheshire Record Office Z/CB/2 9th October 1867.
5   Edward Kemp, *How to Lay Out a Small Garden*. 1850, piv.
6   Cheshire Record Office DPA.
7   Cheshire Record Office Z/CCB/95 Meeting 23rd October 1867.
8   Cheshire Record Office CCF/8/4, 'Verses on The Presentation of the Grosvenor Park to the City of Chester', by J. Housden.
9   Martyn, C. Aylott. 'Some Historic Chester Gardens'. *Cheshire Life*, Volume 10, Number 9, 1944, p10.

Queen's Park, Crewe

*I*n the mid-nineteenth century the Victorians recognised the need to create public parks as a way to manage the burdens of an increasingly urban population and as the century moved on, it was accompanied by a burgeoning number of such parks, with virtually any occasion seeming to be the perfect excuse to open a new one. In June 1888 the London and North Western Railway Company (LNWR) gave Queen's Park to the town of Crewe to mark both Queen Victoria's Jubilee (an event which inspired the opening of many new parks) and also fifty years since the arrival in the town of the Grand Junction Railway. This is recorded in the distinctive lettering around the two park lodges, which reads continuously from the left lodge to the right: 'This park was given by the London & North Western Railway Company to commemorate the Jubilee of her most gracious Majesty Queen Victoria and the 50th anniversary of the opening of the Grand Junction Railway and was opened together with the Victoria Avenue by Field Marshall Commander in Chief HRR The Duke of Cambridge KG on the 9th of June 1888'.

The tradition of industry being seen to care for the public good was a popular one at the time, but local whispering has had it that the reasons behind the creation of Queen's Park were less altruistic, with rumours suggesting that the LNWR Company gave the site to the council in order to persuade them to keep the rival Great Western Railway out of Crewe, thus preserving its precious monopoly.[1] Incidentally, the name of FW Webb appears on the lodge inscription – this is Francis William Webb who was the Chief Mechanical Engineer with the LNWR and became mayor of Crewe in 1887, the same year that the Queen's Park site was presented to the town. The park was Webb's brainchild and it is said that he persuaded the railway directors to donate the land and also £10,000 for laying-out the park.[2]

Thirty-six acres were originally donated and over a hundred years on, Queen's Park is still

Top: Queen's Park boasts a wonderful example of a municipal bandstand.

Later additions to the park include a pergola leading to an aviary, which houses guinea pigs as well as birds.

Queen's Park's many trees make a fine autumn display.

By living in lodges onsite, park keepers can keep an eye out for vandals.

The Central Avenue is lined with silver birches, sycamores & conifers.

a successful example of a well-used and appreciated municipal park.[3] As with any open space, this is largely thanks to the skill of its designer, who in this case was Edward Kemp, who had also designed Grosvenor Park in Chester.

The main feature of Queen's Park is an artificial lake surrounded by a winding path to make a pleasant walk. This was created by scarping the Valley Brook, an ancient stream and also tributary of the river Weaver.[4] The brook at first flowed through the lake but it was used as the town's main sewage outlet as well as its chief source of water and so a problem developed of sewage accumulating in the lake basin until the brook was eventually culverted in 1913.[5] There are still boating facilities and, even on chilly days, the banks are dotted with fishermen's umbrellas. This local pastime has only arisen in recent decades but is not as curious as it may seem since the lake is apparently full of carp and other fish, having been stocked in 1917.[6] The Edwardian park

users even swam in the lake, after a swimming stage was provided in 1912 for local competitions. The lake is not large but it twists and turns so that it cannot all be viewed at once, making it seem a more exciting prospect than it perhaps really is. This impression is aided by three lightly planted islands, one of which can be reached from either side via some rather unattractive mid-twentieth century concrete bridges. Keeping up with significant community issues, this island was relandscaped in the 1960s and now acts as a memorial to the Second World War soldiers who fought in Burma.

These bridges may well find themselves replaced in the near future, thanks to a Heritage Lottery Fund grant of around £2 million, to be used for restoration of the park's original infrastructure, which has gradually deteriorated in recent decades. As Glen Hollier, Grounds Maintenance Superintendent for Crewe and Nantwich Borough Council puts it, cost-cutting in previous decades means that 'ongoing maintenance has always been done but basic infrastructure has deteriorated'. Queen's Park originally enjoyed wooden bridges with knarled rustic timberwork,[7] but the fabric of these was unsuited to the job and so they had disappeared within fifteen years. Allan Leah, landscape architect in the council's planning department, hopes to be able to instate bridges with a similar look to the original ones, but perhaps made of more durable metal. It is also hoped that the expensive but worthwhile process of removing the silt build-up from the lake will be undertaken, which should improve the quality of the water, pleasing the fishermen. One group of park users who will not be pleased however are the troops of geese and other birds who gather on the lake; the original design had herbaceous planting around the lake – now there are simply plain grass

banks – and Allan Leah would like to reinstate this. Geese however are infamous for destroying such plants and so the hope is to be rather more discouraging to these birds in future. On the south bank of the lake there was originally a mound dating from before Kemp's design was imposed on the landscape and this was used in the early days as a viewing platform. Over the years however this has become distorted so that now it is barely noticed.

The walk around the lake and park is stunning in autumn, thanks to the plantings of trees and shrubs. This is largely due to George Latimer, the custodian from 1888-1906, who had a great deal of forestry expertise and therefore planted many of the trees.[8] The original planting was not dense, although in places it has gradually grown more so, and tended to have been planted in small clumps in order to frame a view, or as individual specimens to be

Geese have been very damaging to any plantings around the lake.

admired. Just as the lake cannot be viewed in one go, neither can the rest of the park. The paths are twisting, the planting scattered rather than neatly lined around the outside, and the terrain is undulating, all of which were key parts of Kemp's design principles: 'Where the space will at all justify it, – and it must be restricted indeed if it will not do so, – the walks and plants can be so disposed as to afford as many different views as possible. From no single point, unless it be an elevated one, should every part be seen. A lawn need not be like a bowling-green, with a simple fringe of plantation; but should have a variety of minor glades and recesses, that are only to be discovered and examined from particular points.'[9]

Amongst the largest of the trees at Queen's Park are the silver birches and sycamores which, with conifers, line the Central Avenue in place of the original trees. The Avenue leads proudly from the main entrance to the 1977 Jubilee Cafeteria whose striking twentieth century architecture replaced the original pavil-

ion when it suffered the fate of so many municipal park buildings and burnt down. In front of the cafeteria is another memorial, in full view during the walk up the Avenue but rather cluttered with over-enthusiastic plantings surrounding it. This time a man-sized bronze soldier is mounted on a column with two lions at its base, in recognition of the Boer War.

At the other end of the avenue, at the entrance to the park, stand the two lodges. These are delightful black and white timber framed cottages that would not be out of place in a Grimms fairytale, not least because they carry their own little riddles: the eastern lodge is decorated with a dove, bat and moon, symbolising Sir Richard Moon who was chairman of the LNWR Company, and the western lodge with an olive branch and spider with web,

representing town mayor Webb. The western lodge also has a small bell tower and in between these two buildings, a modest-sized clock tower greets the visitor. One of the chief reasons for the much-bemoaned decline of our municipal parks in recent years has been an increase in vandalism, from which Queen's

Top: One of the islands can be reached via concrete bridges, which may soon be replaced thanks to a Heritage Lottery Fund grant. Middle: Designer Edward Kemp was a great believer in using wing curved paths to create as many views as possible. Bottom: Coronation Walk was laid out to commemorate the crowning of George VI.

*Above: The matching lodges have inscriptions which
read continuously from one to the other.
Below: The ornamental lake can be glimpsed from
many different points in the park.*

Park has not escaped, and one of the chief reasons for the increase in this blight has been a general move towards using contractors to maintain the parks instead of the ever-present park keeper so beloved of childhood comics like the *Beano*. As the park keeper has been phased out, so the lodge in which he would have lived has become vacant, eventually often either falling into disrepair or being sold off perhaps as a private residence. Whilst nevertheless not entirely escaping the vandals, Queen's Park has been very fortunate in retaining its lodges much in the way they were intended. The eastern lodge is still occupied by the widow of a Park Superintendent whose home it was, and the western lodge is soon to be occupied by a Park Ranger who will be able to keep a careful eye on any comings and goings.

'Doing it how it has always been done' is not however always the best policy, a principle which will influence the restoration of the railings around the park. These were added in 1893 after the park's opening and were unusual in that the panels are welded to the posts rather than bolted, with the result that they have rusted and are difficult to repair.[10] In this instance, it may well be a case of 'replacement' rather than 'restoration' as there is a reluctance to perpetuate history's faulty design: it is likely that the railings will be replaced with some in a typical Victorian style, but not that originally chosen for Queen's Park. In addition, during the current reign of health and safety regulations it is likely that any new railings will be higher than the current ones, the spearheads of which are deemed to be dangerously low.

No Victorian park would be complete without a bandstand and fortunately Queen's Park can boast a splendid example, complete with copper cupola, in which band concerts are still played. A second, more modest timber specimen stands on the opposite side of the lake.

In 1937 another royal milestone was marked when the Coronation Walk was laid out by the

The Coronation Walk has grown rampantly
& now provides a rather exciting stroll.

curator at the time, HW Probert, to commemorate the crowning of George VI and Queen Elizabeth. This walk follows a shallow ravine running parallel to the Central Avenue and stretches to the lake from an aviary. Here some friendly guinea pigs and brightly coloured birds live in fear of being stolen, an occurrence to which Glen Hollier refers with a weariness that suggests it has been all too regular. A photograph taken in 1956 for the official guide to Crewe shows the crazy-paving walk lined with small, light plantings of conifers and the like. Today however, the effect is atmospheric and jungly rather than polite and interesting, as the plantings have grown tall and dense, so the thoughts of a stroller down Coronation Walk today tend to be with gnomes and fairies rather than with regal celebrations. The ravine is an original feature of the park, part of a since-lost avenue leading from east to west crossing the end of the main avenue, which is clearly seen in an aerial illustration of the park published in the local newspaper in 1887.[11] Victorians strolling from the bandstand to the pavilion would have used a bridge to cross it but this decayed in the same way as those on the lake. Today, visitors have to follow a steep tarmac path dropping straight down into the ravine and then climbing straight up the other side, a process that is precarious as well as being incongruous in an otherwise gently contoured stroll, but it is hoped that the Heritage Lottery Funded project will enable the reinstatement of the bridge and second avenue.

Select Bibliography

Borough of Crewe, Official Guide. Crewe Borough Council and British Publishing Company Limited, Gloucester, 1956.

Chaloner, WH. *The Social and Economic Development of Crewe, 1780-1923,* Manchester University Press, Manchester, 1950, reprint 1973.

Conway, Hazel. *Public Parks.* Shire Publications, Buckinghamshire, 1996.

English Heritage Register of Parks and Gardens of Special Historic Interest, 1999.

Kemp, Edward. *How to Lay Out a Small Garden.* Bradbury and Evans, London, 1850.

Queen's Park Restoration Management Plan, Final Report, prepared by Bertram Hyde in Association with Clive Payne Consultancy. Crewe & Nantwich Borough Council, January 2001.

References

1   WH Chaloner. *The Social and Economic Development of Crewe, 1780-1923.* 1950, reprint 1973, p90 footnote 1.

2   WH Chaloner. *The Social and Economic Development of Crewe, 1780-1923.* 1950, reprint 1973, p160.

3   *Queen's Park Restoration Management Plan. Final Report,* January 2001, p11.

4   WH Chaloner. *The Social and Economic Development of Crewe, 1780-1923.* 1950, reprint 1973, p2 footnote.

5   WH Chaloner. *The Social and Economic Development of Crewe, 1780-1923.* 1950, reprint 1973, p191.

6   *Queen's Park Restoration Management Plan. Final Report,* January 2001, p15.

7   *Queen's Park Restoration Management Plan. Final Report,* January 2001, plates 6 and 20.

8   *English Heritage Register of Parks and Gardens of Special Historic Interest,* 1999.

9   Edward Kemp. *How to Lay Out a Small Garden.* Bradbury and Evans, London, 1850, p36.

10   *Queen's Park Restoration Management Plan. Final Report,* January 2001, p11.

11   *Queen's Park Restoration Management Plan. Final Report,* January 2001, plate 1.

Mellor's Gardens, Rainow

Gardens are often frivolous things created from huge amounts of money, a love of beautiful extravagances, and a desire to display one's wealth, power and good taste. On the other hand, history also throws up many created with a deeper sense of purpose and 'Mellor's Gardens' at Hough Hole House near Macclesfield are certainly amongst this number. These sincere and humbling gardens were created in the second half of the nineteenth century and are special for having been designed principally in accordance with the route of the phenomenally popular and important seventeenth-century religious narrative, *Pilgrim's Progress*. This was written by the Puritan John Bunyan whilst he was imprisoned for his religious beliefs, and is essentially a Christian allegory in which a pilgrim, appropriately named Christian, travels on a difficult journey from the City of Destruction to the Celestial City, passing along the way places such as the Slough of Despond, the Hill of Difficulty, and the Doubting Castle.

The gardens were created by James Mellor, a Macclesfield cotton manufacturer and farmer whose father had built Hough Hole House at the beginning of the nineteenth century. He was deeply inspired by *Pilgrim's Progress* and by the teachings of eighteenth-century philosopher Emanuel Swedenborg, who taught that the natural world is an allegory of the spiritual one. This outlook is demonstrated by the charming 'Thoughts on a Tuft of Grass' which was written by James Mellor in his book *Occasional Thoughts on Spiritual Subjects*: 'In pulling up a little tuft of grass after the frost had made the soil so that the fibres could draw out almost to their full extent, I found those fibres, or roots, to be a surprising length, I thought these fibres have little mouths, thousands of them busy amongst the soils, gathering their atoms like

Top: The focus of Mellor's Gardens is a shady mill pond.
Inset: According to Pilgrim's Progress, a pair of stone lions guards the Porter's Lodge.

*Mellor's Gardens are not planted with bright flowers,
instead they impress with many shades of green.*

*The gardens slope upwards
away from the house.*

*The Holy Way is represented by a path
of grey stone slates.*

The Porter's Lodge is a simple stone potting shed by a stream.

bees, bringing them to the plant, and so to the light and heat of the Sun, which by Divine aid brings forth what we call grass. This useful and sometimes despised vegetable, plants itself, will grow almost every where, it will grow upon waste and forsaken land, and labours not to have any idle ground; this despised grass is daily bringing its labours to feed cows, sheep, horses, and other animals; this grass will get into higher spheres of life when it has passed through the mouth and four stomachs of the cow, it becomes milk, butter, cheese, and other things for man, at last the flesh of the cow is eaten, whose very horns and hoofs are useful, and all the refuse goes back to its first principles, and there exchanges for larger quantities of food, both for man and beast; thus we find man's body fed by the grass of the field, to which is conjoined a rational soul, the one a native of the Natural world, the other the Spiritual'.[1] Mellor's beliefs were so strong as to even be reflected in his garden, which he called the 'Garden of Correspondence relating to things of this world and Scriptural History',[2] the design of which was essentially dictated by allegory and references to the Bible and *Pilgrim's Progress*. Created by a mind that considers even a tuft of grass with such intensity, we can expect Mellor's Gardens to be something rather special.

In James Mellor's lifetime, and during that of the immediately successive generations, the gardens were open to the public regularly. When he died in 1891, the local paper printed a memoir of his life, together with a sermon for the memorial service which he himself had written, and this recorded the fame of the gardens, as well as the love he poured into them: 'no man ever spent more time and took a greater delight in the peculiar arrangement of a garden and grounds than Mr Mellor did in those of Hough Hole – every nook and corner bears the impress of an industrious hand. "Mellor's Gardens" have been famous for miles around and during the last 50 years have been visited by thousands of spectators.'[3] Unlike many of the gardens in this book, those at

Top: 'The Highway was fenced on either side by a wall'. Bottom: In John Bunyan's tale, Apollyon is a foul fiend and in Mellor's Gardens he is represented by a terracotta fish.

Hough Hole House were built by their owner rather than by their staff or hired help, as James Mellor was apparently handy with a tool and so had his own joiner's shop in which he made the garden's built features, including many little pedestals bearing quotations, scriptural or poetic.[4] Sadly these are now lost.

By the 1920s Hough Hole House was rented to two Miss Russell sisters, who added many plants, such as rhododendrons, to those of Mellor, who used primarily those that are mentioned in the Bible, such as vines and Robinias. The gardens next went into a period of decline until the arrival of Gordon and Ruth Humphries in 1978. With the help of Richard Turner, the Cheshire County Archaeologist, they uncovered Mellor's astonishing garden scheme, which has since been maintained in good condition, having been bought by the Rigby family in the 1990s. Today Hough Hole House is very much a private family home, but its gardens are respected, enjoyed and open to the public twice a year.

Mellor's Gardens are of a distinctly domestic size, which can create an unfortunate element of humour in its recreation of one of our greatest literary and religious epics, but if the visitor can suspend his disbelief, the effect is utterly charming. The route is appropriately difficult to follow, even with a map, which would not have mattered whilst their creator was alive, as the local paper reported that he liked to show visitors around himself: 'Withal the Rainow patriarch was no lugubrious-minded Christian; he had a fund of humour, which he dispersed with a liberal hand according to the dispositions of his visitors, and nothing gave him greater pleasure than to take them through the grounds and explain the meaning of the various names he had given to the respective portions of his rustic demesne'.[5] It begins at the main gate with the premise that wherever the visitor comes from is their own City of Destruction where, if they remain, they will die and 'sink lower than the grave, into a place that burns with fire and brimstone.'[6] From here we cross the Slough of Despond, a

'miry' bog in which Christian begins to sink 'because of the burden [of spiritual anxiety] that was on his back'.[7] This swampy lawn area (once Mellor's vegetable garden)[8] was unsuited to twentieth-century living and so is now a paved area used for car parking, enabling any burdens to be unloaded easily from the car into the house!

We pass through a Wicket Gate to the side of the main house to reach the House of the Interpreter (Mellor's modest stone stables), where Christian is shown things to make him 'stable' in what he has 'begun to take in hand'.[9] Leading up a slope is a steep flight of small steps sunken between dry stone walls to symbolise the passage in *Pilgrim's Progress* where 'the highway was fenced on either side with a Wall and that Wall is called Salvation. Up this way therefore did burdened Christian run'.[10] From this slope leads the Holy Way, a narrow path of grey paving stones to the mill pond that forms the aesthetic focus of the garden as well as representing the Pool of Siloam. Here is a Cross (now broken into a pillar) where Christian loses the burden of his sin into the cave of the Sepulchre, represented by the pond's overflow hole. In its memoir of James Mellor, the *Macclesfield Courier and Herald* tells a funny story which reminds us that this spiritual garden was grounded in reality: 'The overflow from the "pool of Siloam", in which numberless trout disport themselves, runs in a culvert beneath the house. Some 40 years ago a few mischievous Rainow lads determined to grope in the culvert for trout. Mr Mellor had had experience beforehand of their depredations, and was on the look out for the juvenile poachers. When they had got fairly into the culvert and were enjoying their

Inset: James Mellor composed the inscription for his own tomb.

sport, he slipped quietly out by the back door, drew up the paddle of "the Pool of Siloam", and "forth rushed the mighty waters," much to the discomfiture of the poachers, who never again troubled him.'[11] Next to the pool is a delightful white summerhouse, which a plaque above the door claims to be 'Bethel or the House of God'. With glass windows round each of its eight sides, it appears almost like a small watchtower over the pond.

Reaching paths upwards, marked with huge

again, and a small stone lion now represents the pair that in *Pilgrim's Progress* guard the Porter's Lodge. The lodge itself is represented by a plain stone potting shed by the stream feeding the mill pond. Stone slabs form a bridge across and these in fact represent a whole new, if brief, cultural reference – this time *to Uncle Tom's Cabin*, the nineteenth-century American novel that promoted the slave liberation movement, with the bridge representing the shaky ice over which Eliza had to cross with her in-

lush ferns, we are forced to make the same choice as Christian in order to take the correct route from Difficulty, Danger or Destruction. Having hopefully chosen the Hill of Difficulty, we weave our way along a network of paths, managing (unless the day is too warm and sunny!), unlike Christian, to avoid falling asleep at the 'pleasant Arbour' and thus 'indulge the flesh' and 'sleep in the midst of difficulty'.[12]

The path leads back down towards the pond

fant child in order to escape slavery.

From here the path continues along what may appear to be a pleasant route alongside the mill pond, but is actually the Valleys of Humiliation and the Shadow of Death, where 'the pathway was here also exceedingly narrow' with a dangerous quag and very deep ditch (the mill pond) on either side as the embodiment of spiritual doubt.[13] A large terracotta fish decorates the pond, and this represents

Above: The ditch by By-Path Meadow, where
Vain-confidence fell to his death, sprouts lush ferns.

Apollyon, a 'foul fiend' 'clothed with scales' with which Christian has to battle.[14] In *Pilgrim's Progress*, the 'lusty' Vanity-Fair with its attractions of power and sensuality is where Christian has to endure a blow to his pride in a ridiculous and humiliating court case, and in Mellor's Gardens this is represented by the area at the back of what was a mill until converted into part of the house. Next to the pond here is a crude stone slab representing Lot's Wife, who was turned into a pillar of salt for 'look-

to his death. From this lawn Mellor would have had a view of his farmhouse, occupied by a tenant, which represented Doubting Castle in which Christian and Hopeful were imprisoned by Giant Despair. Today this farmhouse is in separate ownership and the view obscured, so the current occupants need no longer feel that they are playing the role of Giant Despair!

We then pass along a grassy slope representing the Delectable Mountains, reaching a surprisingly pretty stone building known as the

ing back with a covetous heart when she was going from Sodom for safety'.[15]

The visitor-pilgrim now moves away from the pond and ascends steps to arrive at By-Path Meadow. This enclosed lawn was used as a tennis court by James Mellor but represents Christian's diversion in which he and Hopeful fall asleep in a meadow 'green all the year long'. To one side is a walled ditch, sprouting exuberant ferns, into which Vain-confidence fell

Howling House. In this innocent setting Mellor recreated the passage from *Pilgrim's Progress* where Christian and Hopeful look into the mouth of Hell at the Valley of the Shadow of Death: 'And ever and anon the flame and smoke would come out in such abundance, with sparks and hideous noises ... also he heard doleful voices, and rushings to and from, so that sometimes he thought he should be torn in pieces.'[16] The house has a cast iron fireplace which could

The Holy Way provides a pleasant route around the gardens,
as well as being an allegory for the Christian journey.

be used to fill the room with smoke, and by adding sulphur the smell was that of brimstone. A sliding panel in the back wall could let in the breeze, which produced atmospheric cries of the tormented from an aeolion harp.

Next to the Howling House are tombs of various members of the Mellor family, including that of James. His inscription was self-composed and reads:

'When I can no longer speak,
Let this stone speak for me,
And say, live near to God,
Carefully read his word, and the
Writings of Swedenborg, you will
See their harmony,
Live accordingly, and you will
Behold wonderful things.'

Nothing in this garden escapes having a double meaning, and this family resting place has the secondary role of representing the graveyard viewed by Christian from Mount Caution, where those men blinded by Giant Despair had blundered against the stones.

We then move down the slope into the Slough of Despond and a deeply sunken path, of almost human-height, to experience Christian's struggle to cross the deep river in which he feared he would die, and felt 'a great darkness and horror'.[17] At last, this path leads to Christian's goal, the Celestial City on Mount Sion. This is Mellor's personal chapel, a simple room with tall thin windows and narrow door, in which he used to preach to congregations.[18] It is set on the first floor of a barn so that it has

140

*James Mellor used to preach to congregations at the
Celestial City, his personal chapel.*

to be reached via an external stone spiral stair-case, representing Christian's steep climb up Mount Sion, which he managed with 'much agility and speed, though the foundation upon which the City was framed was higher than the clouds'.[19] Whilst the garden visitor cannot hope to feel the same feeling of import as Christian on reaching the Celestial City, the 'Paradise of God',[20] it is nevertheless a satisfying moment to have successfully navigated the rather tricky route around the gardens of James Mellor!

Select Bibliography

A Memoir of the late James Mellor of Hough Hole, Rainow (Mellor's Gardens). Reprinted from the Macclesfield Courier and Herald, Claye, Brown and Claye, Macclesfield, 1891.

Askham, Richard. 'Private Eden'. *Cheshire Life*, November 1986, p36-39.

Bunyan, James. *The Pilgrim's Progress*. 1678, Penguin, London, 1965, reprinted with revisions 1987.

English Heritage Register of Parks and Gardens of Special Historic Interest, 1999.

Mellor, James. *Occasional Thoughts on Spiritual Subjects*. Looney and Pilling, Manchester, 1877.

Turner, Richard. *Mellor's Gardens, The Unique Pilgrim's Progress Garden at Hough-Hole House, Rainow, Cheshire*. Macclesfield, Macclesfield and Vale Royal Groundwork Trust, 1989.

Turner, Richard. 'Mellor's Gardens'. *Garden History*, Volume 15, Number 2, 1987, p157-166.

Turner, Richard. *'Mellor's Gardens: A Victorian Allegorical Garden at Hough-Hole House, Rainow, Cheshire'*. Cheshire County Council, Cheshire, 1984.

References

1   James Mellor. *Occasional Thoughts on Spiritual Subjects*. 1877, p51.

2   *A Memoir of the late James Mellor of Hough Hole, Rainow (Mellor's Gardens). Reprinted from the Macclesfield Courier and Herald*, 1891, p5.

3   *A Memoir of the late James Mellor of Hough Hole, Rainow (Mellor's Gardens). Reprinted from the Macclesfield Courier and Herald*, 1891, p3.

4   *A Memoir of the late James Mellor of Hough Hole, Rainow (Mellor's Gardens). Reprinted from the Macclesfield Courier and Herald*, 1891, p6.

5   *A Memoir of the late James Mellor of Hough Hole, Rainow (Mellor's Gardens). Reprinted from the Macclesfield Courier and Herald*, 1891, p5.

6   James Bunyan. *The Pilgrim's Progress*. 1678, 1965, reprinted with revisions 1987, p13.

7   James Bunyan. *The Pilgrim's Progress*, 1678. 1965, reprinted with revisions 1987, p16.

8   *English Heritage Register of Parks and Gardens of Special Historic Interest*, 1999.

9   James Bunyan. *The Pilgrim's Progress*. 1678, 1965, reprinted with revisions 1987, p35.

10 James Bunyan. *The Pilgrim's Progress* 1678, 1965, reprinted with revisions 1987, p35.

11 *A Memoir of the late James Mellor of Hough Hole, Rainow (Mellor's Gardens). Reprinted from the Macclesfield Courier and Herald*, 1891, p8.

12 James Bunyan. *The Pilgrim's Progres*. 1678, 1965, reprinted with revisions 1987, p41.

13 James Bunyan. *The Pilgrim's Progress*. 1678, 1965, reprinted with revisions 1987, p56.

14 James Bunyan. *The Pilgrim's Progress*. 1678, 1965, reprinted with revisions 1987, p51.

15 James Bunyan. *The Pilgrim's Progress*. 1678, 1965, reprinted with revisions 1987, p95.

16 James Bunyan. *The Pilgrim's Progress*. 1678, 1965, reprinted with revisions 1987, p57.

17 James Bunyan. *The Pilgrim's Progress*. 1678, 1965, reprinted with revisions 1987, p137.

18 *A Memoir of the late James Mellor of Hough Hole, Rainow (Mellor's Gardens), Reprinted from the Macclesfield Courier and Herald*, 1891, p5.

19 James Bunyan. *The Pilgrim's Progress*. 1678, 1965, reprinted with revisions 1987, p138.

20 James Bunyan. *The Pilgrim's Progress*. 1678, 1965, reprinted with revisions 1987, p138.

Peover Hall, Knutsford

T he gardens of Peover Hall, near Knutsford, seem to exist in a magical world of their own, one parallel to that in which people bustle about their everyday lives. It is, admittedly, possible that this is simply a confused dream, existing because Peover Hall is hard to find, not being shown on many maps and being marked only by the most discreet of signposts on a little lane between Lower and Upper Peover. In fact, they are hard to pin down not only geographically, but also historically, as surviving archive documents relating to their past are hard to find, making Peover a rather enigmatic landscape where our imagination can run wild, unfettered by historical fact. Adding still further to the haze around Peover is the very design of the gardens, where a series of theatrical compartments create a dramatic effect far removed from the surrounding Cheshire countryside.

What we do know is that Peover was a significant landmark as long ago as the thirteenth century, belonging to the ancient Cheshire family of Mainwaring until 1919. In that year it was sold to the son of a cotton manufacturer, and then again in 1940 to Harry Brooks, a Manchester furniture maker. It now belongs to his son, Randle. The house itself is today a quirky-looking building, consisting of one brick cube with tiny paned windows and pointed gables. This has come about as the result of centuries' worth of curtailed building plans and also demolitions; when it was begun in the sixteenth century, the building was intended to have several branches but in the end only one cross wing was built, which still represents the bulk of the house.[1] Further additions were later made, including a large wing in the eighteenth century, but this was demolished in the 1960s to solve both the problem of architectural disunity, and the poor condition of the building.[2] At this point the current brick façade was also added. This house in fact replaced an earlier one which was further south from that of today. The moat which surrounded it can still be seen, although it now 'protects' rather more humble buildings, such as a saw mill.

Top: Tropaeolum, drapes over the yew framing
Peover Hall's garden compartments.

*Peover Hall is a quirky building with
tiny windows & pointed gables.*

*The spendid seventeenth-century stable block can be
seen even from the inner garden compartments.*

Topiary dominates at Peover, in bold blocky shapes.

With the house now being so curtailed, the stable block dating from 1654 is now almost incongruously splendid, having been built, as is testified by a plaque above the door, as 'The Gift of Mrs Ellen Mainwaring to her Son Thomas Mainwaring Esq 1654'. If only all presents could be that generous! This block has a strangely Tuscan feel with beautifully carved woodwork, ornamental plaster ceiling and generously proportioned stalls. The stable's strangely elevated status is in contrast to the parish church, St Lawrence's, which is so deeply ensconced amongst Peover's pretty estate buildings as to have become a garden feature itself. Indeed, it is now the responsibility of Head Gardener Dave Oldham to look after its churchyard, and as if to emphasise its ornamental role, the entrance is marked with clipped box. Just outside its low walls, in the garden proper, is an avenue of diminutive pleached beech, looking very quaint indeed alongside the brick walls and gravestones of the churchyard.

Over the generations, the designed landscape

of Peover has seen many changes, which has left it with Henry Mainwaring's eighteenth-century landscape park, now rather relaxed but once rather splendid if, as legend has it, it was designed by William Emes. Its gardens today mainly comprise of a network of compartments to the south of the house which were developed in waves of activity, the first being roughly between 1890 and 1905 with Sir Philip Tatton Mainwaring and his wife Emily creating the skeleton of the garden,[3] and the last in the 1960s by current owners Randle and Juliet Brooks.[4] The public visitor enters these by a small gate in the wall and is greeted simply by a wooden honesty box. Peover is open to the public, but only for a few hours a week, in a relaxed 'do come if you fancy it' kind of a way. The first compartment is the

Pink Garden which sits in the crook of the perimeter walls, squeezing in a pergola which supports clematis as well as apple trees. This was designed only in recent decades, although the structure of these compartments is over a century old. From here a brick doorway takes us to what became the White Garden at around the same time. This square garden room is laid

Top: St Lawrence's Church is so integrated as to have almost become a garden feature. Middle: The Lily Pond Garden is dominated by a long loggia. Bottom: All manner of techniques are used to frame different views at Peover.

out with grey paving and box that is clipped into cones and square frames. It is planted with white climbing roses, lilac, agapanthus, choisyas and even grapevines, although the pergola they grew up has recently collapsed, leaving only romantic stone pillars.

Beyond an archway, our attention is grabbed by the Lily Pond Garden, watched over by the church tower on one side, and the stable block on the other. This is contained within yew-hedges and brick walls punctuated with yew 'bookends', and is focussed around a classic rectangular lily pond set deep in a trim grass lawn. Shelter is provided by a long 1920s ve-randah or loggia, almost Roman in appearance,

with stone columns, brick arches and wooden fretwork. The look is a highly-designed one, with large yews clipped into spirals and other shapes, and softened with ferns and plants such as hostas, hydrangeas and geraniums.

Passing from this 'room' through an arch cut into the yew, we reach a Rose Garden which features beds of the eponymous shrub focussed on three paved circles and enclosed within yew hedges through which scarlet tropaeolum squeezes. On one side of the Rose Garden, a gateway cuts through the yew into a corner of the main forecourt to the north of the house. On another side a tunnel is cut through the immense yew, which is topped by clipped

Pleached beech signal the approach to St Lawrence's from the garden.

domes and pierced with 'portholes'. This leads to what is known as the 'Herb Garden', although the herbs were recently removed in order to make space for a marquee needed at a party. The compartment is however still very attractive, criss-crossed with flag paths radiating from the centre, where there is a statue of three small boys. Each of the compartments offers quiet scenes in which to while away the time, and here a seat is offered by a fantastic arbour cut into the yew.

Next to the 'Herb Garden', a tiny wooden door opens out directly from the house onto a handkerchief-sized lawn and a 1980s' knot garden in which box is cut into scrolled shapes, probably best admired from the upstairs of the house. Beyond this is a discreet open-air swimming pool, of course decorated with topiary.

To the front of the house, the garden is more open and simple. The forecourt is defined by a low brick wall, through which plain wooden gates lead out into the rough parkland. Its green lawns are plain but have been planted by the current owners with simple domed and cylindrical yews dotting the lawns, and flowering plants to soften the line of the house. The generous curve of the turning circle was apparently designed in an exuberant moment by Randle Brooks, who ensured that it suited its modern use by drawing the appropriate line with his car.

To the side of this forecourt, taller red brick gateposts lead into larger, stylish, compartments which have striking impact rather than the pretty romance of the previous ones. First is a long lawn, slightly sunken and framed with 1920s' yew hedges. On each side are pretty lines of clipped limes, which were added in the 1960s. Intriguing hints at an earlier garden are

Top: The Theatre Garden uses enclosing green walls to create visual drama. Middle & bottom: The Herb Garden no longer contains any herbs, but can be enjoyed from an arbour cut into the yew. Opposite page: Appropriately, water lilies flourish in the Lily Pond.

provided by older trees such as purple beech and oak. At the end of this walk is the Theatre Garden, the perfect setting for a surreal film. Here tall yew hedges from the 1920s are clipped into boxy shapes and form an enclosed square. This is watched from its own circular yew alcove by a small temple which was only built in 1996, but uses a door pediment from the demolished wing of the house. These compartments have no planting, except for some simple topiary shapes to one side, although bumps in the grass show where there were once flowerbeds. The effect is intense as there are no colours other than many shades of green, serenely blending and contrasting. When trim, the yew provides crisp lines, sometimes straight, sometimes curved, but always dramatic.

If the yew compartments are theatrical, then there is certainly a behind-the-scenes area, where the gardens have slipped into a relaxed, rambling mode. Here is a huge walled garden, which is largely the domain of the Brooks' hyperactive pet dogs, who rush to yap at the ankles of any passer-by who innocently opens the door. Dated at around the eighteenth century,[5] this area is now barely productive and the remaining peach tree in the glasshouse struggles to bear fruit under cracked and broken glass. The Ordnance Survey map from 1877 however shows this garden laid out in four quarters, divided by lines of small trees, and one quarter is filled, presumably as an orchard.[6] This same map also shows a circular walk that winds its way through trees around the edge of the gardens, and this too still exists in places.

Below the walls of the kitchen garden is a sunken dell with an azalea rockery to one side and small pool edged with purple irises at its bottom. Here the formal and the informal compete for the upperhand as the naturalistic hollow is reached by descending a flight of steps that brim with import but also with moss. On the either side of the steps run straight lines of box each capped by large yew domes, which struggle to break free from their clipped shapes.

This unlikely corner perhaps conveys the essence of Peover today. A high maintenance design that demands attention and strict discipline has not rebelled entirely from its regime, but has certainly decided to relax and have a little fun. Peover feels, to me, like a garden that could leap to attention at any moment but in the meantime is enjoying life in its own slightly surprising private world.

A simple swimming pool is embellished with a modern knot garden.

*A small temple, built from the door pediment of a demolished wing
of the Hall, entices the visitors into the Theatre Garden.*

Select Bibliography

English Heritage Register of Parks and Gardens of Special Historic Interest, 1999.
Laurie, Ian. 'Peover in perspective'. *Cheshire Life*, Volume 51, 5th May 1985, p36-37.
Montgomery-Massingberd, Hugh. 'Peover's progress of the Mainwarings'. Reprint from *The Field*, 2nd
March 1985.
Ordnance Survey 25" to 1 mile, Cheshire Sheet 35.10, 1st edition 1877.

References

1   *English Heritage Register of Parks and Gardens of Special Historic Interest*, 1999.
2   Hugh Montgomery-Massingberd. 'Peover's progress of the Mainwarings'. Reprint from *The Field*,
     2nd March 1985.
3   Ian Laurie. 'Peover in perspective'. *Cheshire Life*, Volume 51, 5th May 1985, p36.
4   *English Heritage Register of Parks and Gardens of Special Historic Interest*, 1999.
5   *English Heritage Register of Parks and Gardens of Special Historic Interest*, 1999.
6   *Ordnance Survey 25" to 1 mile*, Cheshire Sheet 35.10, 1st edition 1877.

Ness Botanic Gardens, the Wirral

A common complaint amongst garden history enthusiasts is that whilst they are originally attracted to the subject from their love of gardening and horticulture, they soon find it to be a field dominated by discussions of design and architecture, where plants are given relatively little attention. Ness Botanic Gardens on the Wirral will be a treat for these complainants, as design is here forced to take a backseat behind its thousands of plants. The design of the gardens constantly evolves and as such they are not at first glance particularly historic, but the role they have played in the development of horticulture certainly does earn them a place in history. This rather unassuming hillside garden was in fact a major force behind the introduction of many of the plants that we now take for granted in this country.

The gardens at Ness were begun in the early decades of the twentieth century as the pet project of a gentleman by the name of Mr Arthur Kilpin Bulley. In order to appreciate the warmth of feeling behind Ness, it is important to appreciate the remarkable character of Arthur Bulley. History has accorded him the reputation of being a independent thinker: a wealthy socialist who was benevolent, open-minded, and forward-thinking and who stood in the January 1910 Parliamentary election as a Women's Suffrage candidate, polling 639 votes.[1]

Bulley had been obsessive about plants for many years, cramming a domestic garden in West Kirby full of unusual species. These he obtained by careful networking, probably employing many of the same business skills he used in his careers as first a broker and then a

Top: The army of plants at Ness provides a show in any season, especially in the Rock Garden. Inset: Musa basjoo musuceae.

A Japanese Banana looms over a corner of the terraces.

Ness is full of quiet corners to explore.

The Rock Garden is composed of an intricate network of paths & pools.

Curtains on the terrace walls protect plants from cold weather.

Above left: Arthur Bulley's family house at Ness. Above right: Bulley cultivated a profitable friendship & correspondence with the Regius Keeper of the Royal Botanic Garden, Edinburgh (Ness Botanic Gardens).

merchant of cotton. His particular interest was in alpines, which were only recently being recognised as potential occupants of English gardens, and he spent the 1890s building an impressive plant collection. This was achieved through a campaign of catalogue ordering and networking which included exchanging seeds and notes with the new botanic garden at Kew, and even persuading missionaries in China to bring him back unusual seeds! Arguably the most significant link in the network he created at this time was the friendship he built with Professor Isaac Bayley Balfour, the Regius Keeper of the Royal Botanic Garden, Edinburgh, and holder of the grand title of 'Queen's Botanist in Scotland'. Balfour and Bulley were to exchange advice and seeds for decades to come – if only we could all have such horticultural experts as penfriends!

It was in 1898 that the need for a larger garden drove Mr Bulley and his wife to move to a newly-built but largely unremarkable family home on Micklewell Brow. The site had previously been an open space in public use, but Bulley began to convert the fields and rough gorse-covered land to the form which would become famous as Ness Botanic Gardens. Given its exposed position overlooking the Dee estuary at fifty-seven metres above sea level, an early job was to plant shelter belts, but to the south of the house was a valley that acted as a sun-trap. Bulley tried to create a rock garden here but the clay soil was so heavy that this was not a great success.[2] Nearby he con-

structed a lengthy pergola, which has long since collapsed, but some of the plants that grew up it have survived on today's terraces. Also created were azalea beds, a shrub section, and an exuberant herbaceous garden, with different borders for each month. Over the course of the Second World War this, with much of Bulley's gardens, fell into decay and was subsequently replaced.

Bulley did not simply create his gardens for his private enjoyment however. As he was a socialist even in his horticulture, his garden was from the beginning open to the public and for this reason was never designed to integrate with the house, unlike those at Tirley Garth, for example, which are very much intended to radiate out from the main building to complement and be enjoyed from it. In addition, his passion for seed exchanges grew in 1904 into a nursery business – Bees Limited (early on named 'Co-operative Bees Limited') – with the expressive motto 'All to Gather, All together'.[3] Whilst thriving thanks to Bulley's innate business sense, this was also a way in which to share seeds, with 'every-gardener' being able to purchase them through Woolworths shops. Bees was for many years actually based at Ness and exploited areas such as its herbaceous borders as a catalogue marketing tool, with one of the two long brick buildings remaining today near the glasshouses, being used as the packing shed.[4] So Ness Gardens and Bees Limited flourished, so much so in fact that by 1907 the whole

Above: Bulley built his house on open land & gradually connected the fields to garden. The area shown here now largely occupied by the terraces & Rock Garden (Ness Botanic Gardens).

enterprise employed fifty-two garden staff, bringing the wage bill to £50 a week.[5] Arthur Bulley was a charismatic person and so the gardens in many ways became the focus of the local community, with much of the workforce coming from the neighbourhood. Not only did Bulley make provision for public sports areas such as a bowling green (now the Sorbus Lawn) and tennis courts (now the Herb Garden), but he even allowed those locals without baths to wash in his house.[6]

In 1911 Bees moved to its own site at Sealand, near Chester, and so Bulley was able to redesign the gardens with an ornamental role and to this end employed a new Head Gardener, Josiah Hope, who came on the recommendation of Mr Balfour from the botanic garden at Edinburgh. With Hope's help Bulley did now achieve his thwarted aim of a rock garden, bringing in top soil from building works in the village and creating raised beds. The collection of alpine plants used mass planting techniques and flourished and grew famous, reflecting Bulley's presence in the gardening world beyond his own back gate. Mr Hope also flourished at Ness, in spite of his masonic Conservatism being somewhat at odds with the politics of his employer, and became one of its longest standing staff members. He was even exempted from being enlisted in the First World War after Bulley repeatedly wrote that he was needed at Ness to grow food for the war effort.[7]

Over the Victorian period the world had opened up to Europe as travel and enterprise through a globe largely ruled by Britain became easier. Foreign treasures were the subject of great fascination and passion and many hoards were brought home to Britain from the far corners of the earth. Plants were at the top of many a gentleman's shopping list and a tradition of plant hunting arose in which brave scientific and horticultural men explored remote places in order to bring back new excitements for western gardens. In particular, East Asia was plundered for its botanical wealth and the plants of this area, including camellias, wisteria, jasmine and rhododendrons, are now so familiar and central to our gardens that it is hard to imagine that they were once considered foreign. By the beginning of the twentieth-century, the demand had become so intense that a new generation of professional plant-hunters arrived in East Asia. From his garden on the Wirral, Arthur Bulley was a key figure in this movement, using his wealth to fund several of the most important plant hunters on their expeditions, and thus overcoming the inherent limitations of networking and catalogues in order to obtain seeds.

Bulley's first foray into sponsorship was in 1904 when he hired Scotsman George Forrest to travel to Rangoon to collect seeds from alpines and hardy herbaceous plants in the North West Yunnan mountains. Forrest was recommended by Balfour, having worked for him in a sedate job in the RBG Edinburgh's herbarium.[8] Famously working in extremely

difficult and dangerous conditions with threats from wild animals and unfriendly tribesmen, Forrest was able to bring back the *Pieris formosa forrestii* whose red leaves and white bell flowers are so beloved of our gardens today. Ness contains a huge and spectacular example of this shrub, which was actually raised from Forrest's original batch of seed. Current Head Gardener Paul Cook laughingly acknowledges the responsibility of looking after such a historic shrub, agreeing that its death would be the stuff of nightmares. In fact, previous curator Peter Cunnington did see it 'turn all brown' following a particularly heavy frost in the early 1980s. It was cut right down to the ground and lived to see another day, although it has now perhaps become a 'basis plant', sprouting new growth and thus becoming somewhat of a new specimen. He also brought back the beautiful blue trumpets of *Gentiana sino-ornata*, for which Ness is famous, and in addition we have the Forrest-Bulley partnership to thank for many rhododendrons such as *Rhododendron roxieanum*, and new species of primu-

las, such as the *Primula bulleyana* which was named after Forrest's sponsor. However, difficulties were eventually caused as tensions arose between employer and employee and so Forrest found himself a new sponsor.[9] He still holds a place in Ness's heart however and a new alpine garden is being created near the greenhouses to mark the centenary of Forrest's first foray into plant hunting.

Looking for someone to fill the gap left by George Forrest, Bulley was recommended Frank Kingdon Ward, again by Balfour. Already working in Shanghai as a teacher, but with a taste for exploration, Kingdon Ward in January 1911 accepted the challenge to travel to the Yunnan and Tibetan marshes.[10] Kingdon Ward brought back many plants, including the

Rhododendron pemakoense, but they were often felt to be of greater scientific than gardening interest, a frustrating situation for Bees, which was now locked into rivalry with Veitch's Nursery to introduce better plants to the eager gardening public. During this period however, Bees did still continue to attain greater and greater acclaim, winning many medals for its plants.

Wanting still more primulas and also hardy herbaceous plants, Bulley next employed Roland Edgar Cooper to go to Sikkim, between Nepal and Bhutan, in 1913. Cooper discovered some tiny primulas but whilst an exciting find, these proved to be difficult to grow in the United Kingdom, and not suitably showy for the popular gardening market. To add to the disappointment, Kew at this time was in-

Top: Gaultheria. Middle: Gentiana sino-ornata. (P. Cunnington).
Bottom: Nerines provide a splash of colour.

undated with specimens and so actually returned the samples that Bulley had always been
in the habit of sending.[11] In 1914 however
Cooper targeted Bhutan and was rewarded
with the clustered ivory flowers of *Primula
eburnea* (also known as *Primula harroviana*),
which in 1919 won the Royal Horticultural
Society's Award of Merit.

When the First World War came however
Cooper was enlisted and Bees had to reflect
public demand by stocking seeds for vegetables
rather than flowers, actually closing some of
its plant and florist shops. Bulley tightened the
purse strings, ceasing intense sponsorship of
plant collecting except in 1919 when he helped
to fund the celebrated rock garden enthusiast
Reginald Farrer on a trip to Upper Burma.
Farrer found *Nomocharis farreri* but sadly this
trip was to be his last as he died in the Burmese
hills of ill health.[12]

The roll call of plant hunters that Bulley spon-
sored is impressive, to say the least. Forrest,
Kingdon Ward, Cooper and Farrer are all inter-
nationally celebrated and there are few
gardens in the Western world that have not
benefitted from their introductions. In
particular, having been launched by Arthur
Bulley, George Forrest continued to collect for
the rest of his life, eventually introducing many
primulas, camellias, *Mahonia lomarrifolia* with
its distinctive scented yellow flowers and jagged
leaves, and hundreds of rhododendrons, in
addition to the *Gentiana sino-ornata*. During
his career, again begun by Bulley, Frank Kingdon
Ward brought back many more rhododendrons
and primulas, as well as supplying the seeds first

used to cultivate the currently popular blue
Himalayan poppy, *Meconopsis betonicifolia*.
With these pedigrees, there can be no doubt that
Arthur Bulley was a key player in the cut-and-
thrust of plant collecting.

Bulley died in 1942 and six years later his
daughter Lois presented their home to the University of Liverpool, a fitting owner for so
important a garden. Ness had suffered during
the Second World War so work needed to be
done, and in 1957 Director Ken Hulme was
appointed, beginning to redesign Bulley's compartments into the relatively naturalistic
lay-out that is present today. In recent decades
Ness has continued to evolve, which is
appropriate for a garden in which horticultural
progress was always prioritised over issues such
as design. Pine Wood (the stretch of woodland
running down the side of the gardens) is
relatively old, being an original shelter belt, and
the Specimen Lawn, with its fine shrubs and
trees was opened to the public by Bulley, but
the border of rhododendrons is more of a new-
comer, having been formed after the Second
World War. Pine Wood is Paul Cook's favourite
part of the garden, because: 'it's got an atmosphere. It was one of the areas planted by Bulley
so it shows the current mix between Bulley's
ideas of how the garden would develop and
Ken Hulme's plantings. Things have happened
there and it has now reached maturity, plus, it
has views of the Estuary too.' Features such as
the Heather Garden and Laburnum Arch are
now so synonymous with Ness that it is hard
to believe they are relatively recent additions,
with the heather being introduced in 1961 and

Above left: Pieris formosa forrestii (P. Cunnington).
Above right: Cortaderia selloana 'Sunningdale Silver'.

the Arch in the 1970s. The much-loved sandstone terraces, which are planted with fuschias and hypericums as well as more unusual plants such as an exuberant Japanese Banana *(Musa basjoo musuceae)* were built in the 1960s and 70s and the Belvedere above the Rock Garden commemorates May Gertrude Davidson, a benefactor. The design here is now in a very different form from the early attempts to create a rock garden, being laid out with a gentle stream, bridges, and naturalistic beds containing an array of plants from primulas, to ferns, to grasses. Beyond here is a newly-created woodland garden but an older element is represented in the unusual name of 'Pingo', the lightly wooded area to the west. This dates back even before Bulley's day when it referred simply to the enclosed field there. The waterfall was only constructed in 1996 and it was only in the 1970s that the Water Garden in the valley below took on its pretty form with varied trees surrounding pools, having previously been used for scientific research.

Behind all this, the original principles supporting Ness still stand firm. Its 'Friends', one of the first of such groups to be founded, are key to the garden's management, an example of 'co-operative' working of which Bulley would have approved. It is also the site of a great deal of serious scientific research, pushing horticultural boundaries just as Bulley had in the previous century. Bulley's legacy is felt strongly by Paul Cook who enjoys work at Ness partly because of its inclusive *raison d'être*.

Next time you look around Ness Botanic Gardens, do enjoy the many plants and flowers but try also to look beyond them and picture how Ness is not only a botanical jewel in its own right, but also a crucial player in the plant hunting movement that built the horticultural jewellery box enjoyed by the whole of the United Kingdom.

Select Bibliography

Campbell-Culver, Maggie. *The Origin of Plants.* Headline, London, 2001.
Cooper, RE, Curle, AO, Fair, WS ed. *George Forrest, VMH.* The Scottish Rock Garden Club, Edinburgh, 1935.
Cox, EHM. *Farrer's Last Journey: Upper Burma, 1919-20.* Dulau & Co. Ltd, London, 1926.
English Heritage Register of Parks and Gardens of Special Historic Interest, 1997.
Hulme, JK. *Ness Gardens: Bulley's beginnings to the present day.* Ness Garden, Ness, 1987.
Kingdon Ward, Frank. *The Land of the Blue Poppy: Travels of a Naturalist in Eastern Tibet,* Cambridge University Press, 1913.
Lemmon, Ken. 'Haven for Far Eastern Treasure'. *Country Life,* 19th April 1984, p1058-60.
McLean, Brenda. *A Pioneering Plantsman: A.K. Bulley and the Great Plant Hunters.* HMSO, London, 1997.
Rothwell, Nancy. *Ness Botanic Gardens: Guide Book.* The University of Liverpool, Liverpool, c1995.

References

1   JK Hulme. *Ness Gardens: Bulley's beginnings to the present day.* 1987, p12.
2   JK Hulme. *Ness Gardens: Bulley's beginnings to the present day.* 1987, p4.
3   Brenda McLean. *A Pioneering Plantsman: A.K. Bulley and the Great Plant Hunters.* 1997, p22.
4   *English Heritage Register of Parks and Gardens of Special Historic Interest*, 1997.
5   Brenda McLean. *A Pioneering Plantsman: A.K. Bulley and the Great Plant Hunters,* 1997, p53.
6   JK Hulme. *Ness Gardens: Bulley's beginnings to the present day.* 1987, p27.
7   Brenda McLean. *A Pioneering Plantsman: A.K. Bulley and the Great Plant Hunters,* 1997, p54.
8   RE Cooper, AO Curle, WS Fair ed. *George Forrest, VMH.* 1935, p12.
9   Brenda McLean. *A Pioneering Plantsman: A.K. Bulley and the Great Plant Hunters.* 1997, p77.
10 Frank Kingdon Ward. *The Land of the Blue Poppy: Travels of a Naturalist in Eastern Tibet.* 1913, preface.
11 Brenda McLean. *A Pioneering Plantsman: A.K. Bulley and the Great Plant Hunters.* 1997, p93.
12 EHM Cox. *Farrer's Last Journey: Upper Burma, 1919-20.* 1926, p88.

Thornton Manor and Port Sunlight, the Wirral

G ardens shoot from the most unlikely of sources, and Port Sunlight and Thornton Manor
on the Wirral demonstrate this impeccably, as both have grown from something as non-
horticultural as soap. Behind the creation of both soap and gardens was a gentleman by
the name of William Hesketh Lever, who was born in 1851 into a Bolton grocer's
family. He went on to set up a company that found great success making Sunlight
soap, which was manufactured first in Warrington and then on the Wirral once
expansion called for better transport links. So much success in fact, that he became
a very wealthy man – we have only to note that the name of William Lever is now
represented in the corporate title 'Lever Fabergé', who make household items ranging
from washing powder to deodorant, to appreciate quite how profitable his company
became. In fact, whilst the name 'Lever' has continued, William's own title evolved
into 'Lord Leverhulme', as he was made a Viscount in recognition of his achievements
and also absorbed his wife's surname, Hulme.

   In spite of being a successful businessman, Lever was not only interested in making
a quick profit, and developed a strikingly rounded and benevolent attitude towards his
employees, although he always insisted that this was purely an application of the business principle that a happy workforce meant a productive workforce. This attitude
was reflected in things like the implementation of employee shares, healthcare provision for staff, pension schemes,[1] and most significantly in the construction from 1889
onwards of a purpose-built staff village, to ensure a good quality of life for his employees. This was named Port Sunlight after the product it served and was inspired by
the principle that people are happiest in a good environment, which Lord Leverhulme

*Top: Thornton Manor's main door, through a circular
forecut, is surprisingly small for such a large house.*

*Inset: Many of the statues at Thornton Manor were auctioned
separately from the house following Lord Leverhulme's death*

himself explained in a horticultural metaphor: 'if you provide the right soil to grow in, and plenty of good fresh air and bright and happy conditions, you can produce good flowers; and just as the rose can be produced by healthy surroundings, so living in a healthy village … stimulates to a greater interest in the dull monotonous route of life in a great industry and makes for superior human happiness and well being'.[2] Such quality of life as Leverhulme aimed for was in marked contrast to the terrible living and working conditions that had become the norm for the lower classes in nineteenth-century Britain.

Port Sunlight, which has barely changed since its completion in 1914, is an almost unbearably pretty model village, in which one imagines the inhabitants live a charmed utopian life. In 1907, the author of *Engines of Social Progress*, WL George, declared that Lever's village was an 'unqualified success': 'Nothing is forgotten, nothing is left to chance; the wheels within wheels revolve slowly and regularly without the suggestion of a jar'.[3] Here, the architectural and operational jumble created by the piecemeal development of most British towns is absent and instead this village is impeccably planned. Every detail has been thought through, seen even in the way that the cottages near the railway line do not have their backs to it in the Victorian style, but rather their front lawns cheerfully face it full on in order to impress the passing rail travellers.[4]

The core of Port Sunlight is its still-operational factory, the workings of which are

screened by a smart red brick façade, which opens out onto tree-lined streets that even today are free of any significant traffic. Lever supplied cosy cottages in a joyful assortment of nostalgic architectural designs, all of which are quaintly 'chocolate box'. Each is fronted by a small garden, sometimes communal, with more significant spots, such as in front of the timber framed Post Office, being marked with flowerbeds.

At first, Lever allowed the residents to each maintain their own front garden, as well as providing allotments, but when the results turned out to be decidedly lacking in any uniformity, the railings were removed and the company took over responsibility for maintenance. Writing in *Civic Art*, the influential landscape architect Thomas Mawson explained: 'The arrangement and working of the gardens is admirable, and in practice works exceedingly well. Everyone who has endeavoured to secure a beautiful village knows the difficulty of securing uniformity of cultivation and tidiness. This difficulty is met by letting the allotment gardens in separate tenancies, the groups of houses are erected, the gardens facing the streets being in charge of the estate gardeners, the cottagers paying three pence per week for this service. The one drawback of this system is that it lacks the individual charm of the old-fashioned borders of perennials under each cottage window, which give character to so many old-world villages.'[5] Generally though, Lever was a great believer in the value of gardening, saying in an address to the Agricultural and Horticultural

Top: The Lady Lever Art Gallery was built as a posthumous tribute to the first Lord Leverhulme's wife. Bottom: In front of the Lady Lever Art Gallery is a formal pool with fountain.

Association in 1912: 'We have a great deal in common. We are great believers in gardens. The persons living in the houses we have at Port Sunlight have the option of having a garden, and I find that nearly all have gardens. Some prefer to keep poultry, and so on, but all have the option of having a piece of land'.[6] Today the cottages of Port Sunlight are largely privately-owned, but the estate as a whole, an early 'garden suburb', is managed by the Port Sunlight Village Trust, which ensures that the integrity and uniformity of the design is upheld.

Provision was also made for public open spaces, both formal and informal, including boulevards and bowling greens. Using the hollow of a tidal channel, a sunken Dell provides a ten minute stroll through naturalistic landscaping as it winds from north to south, passing under a sandstone bridge along the way. Reached by descending stone steps from the road, this grassy cranny is planted with shrubs and trees and generously bestowed with benches so that residents can enjoy the peace and quiet. Providing a showy alternative are the 'Diamond' and the 'Causeway', long formal gardens planted with rows of trees and beds of roses. The two designs intersect at a nobly-sized First World War memorial, to which steps ascend having passed through white roses whose smell is so intoxicating as to be still enjoyable many metres away. Watching over this and fronted by a formal pool with fountain, is the Lady Lever Art Gallery, which was built between 1913 and 1922 as a posthumous tribute to Lord Leverhulme's wife.

Having appreciated the beautiful surroundings that Lever provided for his workforce, we inevitably wonder what kind of home he enjoyed himself. In 1888 he rented what was then a nondescript Victorian villa some ten miles from Port Sunlight, Thornton Manor, before actually buying it in 1891.[7] That he was a dynamic 'get it done' man is witnessed in the creation of a network of tree-lined avenues stretching from Thornton Manor to Port Sunlight, amongst other places, which he used as private roads to ensure efficient travel for himself. The gated beginning of one of these roads can still be seen outside the Manor, although it is later dissected by the M53.

Lever hired several architects, including Douglas & Fordham and James Lomax Simpson to transform the Victorian villa into a new house in a more contemporary style.[8] Nearby he constructed Thornton Hough, another model village, but this time without a factory. To transform the grounds, he employed the landscape architect Thomas Mawson. In his autobiography, Mawson recounts an amusing story of how they met, with Lever writing to him after Mawson had sought a donation for his church work. Lever wrote: 'Now that you have had the courage to ask me for a subscription, may I be so bold as to ask you to come and advise me upon the improvement of my garden at Thornton Manor? I have wanted to consult you for the last two years, but all my friends warned me that it would be useless, as you never worked for anyone holding less social rank than a Duke, whereas I am only a poor and indigent soapmaker.'[9] Lever brimmed with ideas for his gardens and the

159

Above: The cottages of Port Sunlight are built in many different styles, all of them pretty.

project was very much a collaboration,[10] being so successful that, by the time work ended, the gardens had grown so large that the house had had to be extended in order to maintain its proportions. Mawson went on to work at Lever's other houses in London (The Hill, Hampstead) and Lancashire (Roynton Cottage, Rivington Gardens), with the partnership only ending in 1912 after Lever felt that Mawson had become too busy to pay him sufficient attention.[11] Over his career Mawson worked on impressive public projects such as the Palace of Peace at the Hague, as well as private gardens like those of Henry Gladstone at Burton Manor. Like the house, the gardens Mawson created were in a new style from that of the earlier nineteenth century. Almost inevitably, the Victorian love of exuberant display and welcoming of mass production had led many to react passionately, leading to the 'Arts and Crafts' movement which promoted traditional values and creative design, in fields from furniture making and textiles, to architecture and gardens, thus reuniting the two values of 'arts' and 'crafts'. In garden design the Arts and Crafts style was typically a romantic look, suggestive of the past, in which

flowering, cottage-style plants were grown informally in a design structured by rustic stonework, pergolas, loggias, terraces and small pools. Gone was the showy pomp of the Victorians and in was a new look that somehow managed to be unmistakeably English whilst at the same time being reminiscent of Italy, throwing aside the values of earlier generations whilst relentlessly harking back to the past. Thomas Mawson was a leading figure of Arts and Crafts and so Lord Leverhulme's gardens and house are a fine example of this style, having remained relatively unchanged over the following century.

Thornton Manor remained the property of the Leverhulme family until the last Viscount, grandson of the first, died in 2000. He was without male heir to whom he could pass the title, and none of his three daughters wanted to live at Thornton Manor, so it was decided to sell the house and have Sothebys auction its contents. Following a difficult period of uncertainty, especially for the staff, it was sold to property developers Lee and Janet Magner to be made into an upmarket health spa. High standards were maintained during the last Viscount Leverhulme's lifetime, with eight

The stable block at Thornton Manor may soon be converted into flats.

gardeners as well as an array of household staff including butlers and chauffeurs. Following the Viscount's death however the house was mothballed and the gardens kept merely 'ticking over', with three gardeners being the only staff to remain. This suspension of time will continue until the arduous process of planning applications is over and work begins on the spa, probably in 2004.

The splendour of Thornton Manor is understated and so having left the road to pass under a black and white gatehouse, the visitor finds himself immediately in the circular forecourt fronting the house's main door, itself no bigger than that of the average terraced home, although rather more attractive. This walled area is framed with climbing roses and colourful borders and to one side a semi-circular alcove leads directly into the main gardens. The effect of these are immediate and striking with a huge long formal terrace under open skies, overlooking the fields below. During the lifetime of the last Viscount, Philip, these were filled with his beloved horses, but they are thought to have perhaps been originally used for golf.

With the first Lord Leverhulme's compulsion for activity in mind, a circular walk was created which loops around the fields, always with a view of the house. This begins at one end of the main terrace as a smart gravel path with sprawling conifers and a sequence of steps so spread out as to make the descent almost unnoticeable. At the bottom is a secluded area known as 'the Dell', where tranquil pools of lilies rest in lush green grass sheltered by dainty cherry trees. Nearby is a small cricket pavilion, but the pitch has not now been used within living memory and the grass waves at knee high. From here the going is rougher and there are no real opportunities to sit, as Lever was a great believer in the value of hard work.[12]

Regrettably, anyone undertaking this circuit today arrives eventually at a leylandii hedge of monstrous appearance and proportions, being so large as to absolutely dominate the view from the house. There is however a small opening through the foliage, and this leads to a rather lost lake. This was once an integral part of Mawson's design, a major feature and also an important focus of the view from the house. Public right of way however demands that a footpath pass through the property between the paddock and the lake, a problem which was originally dealt with by sinking the footpath in an immense ditch so that ramblers would pass through the garden unseen and unseeing, and the lake could be reached by a little footbridge. In recent years, Lord Leverhulme began to feel that even this complex arrangement did not give enough privacy, so the ditch was planted on either side with the leylandii. The unfortunate effect of this is that the connection between the lake, garden and house has been lost, which is particularly inappropriate given the Arts and Crafts emphasis on linking the house with its surroundings. Indeed, following the sale of the house and main gardens, the lake has remained the property of the Leverhulme estate, further detaching it from the rest of the design.

Originally, this now wild lake was well-maintained with trim grass banks, a canal leading to an open-air swimming pool, and islands planted with rhododendrons.[13] To one corner was an immense boathouse which had a social role as much as a practical one. A black and white photograph of this was published in Thomas Mawson's *The Art and Craft of Garden Making*, showing a low, long rustic building which is papered with trellis and has an almost Swiss look. Mawson described this building: 'with wet and dry docks, repairing shops and stores, and the rooms all arranged on a scale adapted to the needs of large parties taking part in aquatic sports also, for which the owner, Lord Leverhulme, catered so liberally.'[14] Sadly, in recent decades this was vandalised by local children and then pulled down. Today, from the empty footprint of the boathouse, one can still pick a way through undergrowth, up mossy overgrown steps, and back into the garden proper.

The terrace overlooking the paddocks is at the heart of the 'garden proper' and at the centre of this is a huge open section, which is

smartly paved with straight walkways linking octagonal sections. The house opens out onto this terrace via a large loggia, which is accessed directly from the dining room to enable *al fresco* eating. Whilst the terrace itself feels very open, the loggia has a restful, enclosed feel created by walkways of limes which shield but do not hide the terrace beyond. A blurring of the distinction between indoor and outdoor is a distinguishing feature of Thornton Manor, and indeed of the Arts and Crafts style. The first Lord Leverhulme went so far as to have an open air bedroom so that he could not only eat in the fresh air of the loggia, but even sleep in the fresh air as well.

Just as people are sent outdoors to admire the garden, plants are brought indoors in a delightfully tiny fernery which is now accessed by a small wooden door in the service wing. Squeezed as it is between the house walls, this cranny feels less like an intentionally designed feature than a disused storeroom in which plants have spotted and seized an opportunity to reclaim a corner of the house for themselves. The fernery is now rather dilapidated as the creeping fig begins to take over, but the goldfish in the pools still swim as happy as larry. Less fortunate was a conservatory on the terrace, which decayed and was then demolished in recent decades, being replaced by an unsatisfactory garden designed by local schoolchildren.

To the south-eastern end of the terrace are

Top left: There were once many statues at Thornton Manor, but now few remain.
Top right: A long terrace stretches across the Manor, & at one end is a stone pavilion.
Opposite page: The Dell offers peace in a natural setting, away from the house.
Below: An open terrace looks over fields once used as horses' paddocks.

planted neat lines of clipped lime trees to form pleasant shaded walks over careful paving patterns leading to a stone pavilion. To the north is what is known as 'the Forum'. In this striking area a rectangular lawn with a huge classical urn is enclosed by concrete pillars, which in turn are framed by flower borders and a straight path punctuated with those statues that were not auctioned. Photographs in Mawson's autobiography show that the pillars would have been practically bare, and the spaces between them filled with planted trellis, with further wooden supports creating a rose pergola.[15] Over the years the trellis has been lost and instead the pillars act as a support for ivy as well as the roses which, as current gardener Nick Lightfoot observes, is probably fortunate given that many of the pillars are inevitably crumbling with age and in need of attention. It is hoped that such care will be forthcoming in the next few years as, clearly, the gardens will be a huge draw to potential spa guests.

Beyond the Forum, steps lead down to a smooth green croquet lawn, although part of this is taken up with a now defunct hard-surface tennis court. Further north again, steps descend to a circular Rose Garden, although this now relies more on plants like fuschias than roses. Reminiscent of an amphitheatre, this area has banked sides and is given unusual dramatic effect by the presence of a huge boulder, which in 1995 was made into a water feature as an eightieth birthday gift from the estate's staff and pensioners. This garden is flanked by enclosed square lawns which are framed by shrubs and rose arches. Further north again, more naturalistic planting pockets lead downwards towards some remaining statues and the grandly titled 'arboretum', in which are planted trees given to Lord Leverhulme in 1997 as a thank you for his contributions towards the University of Liverpool.

This whole can be admired from the balustraded roof of a long stone loggia on the croquet lawn. This was designed not by Mawson, but by James Lomax Simpson, who is also responsible for part of the house.[16] The view from the other side of the roof is currently a rather less inspiring one of the sizeable walled kitchen garden which is now an empty waste ground but was once practical and also decorative, being reachable through a doorway in the back of the loggia. In *The Art and Craft of Garden Making* Thomas Mawson wrote of this pleasure role: 'Here the primary object was to provide sheltered walks convenient to the residence and connecting directly with the principle terrace walks.'[17] He accompanies this with a plan[18] and photograph[19] that show it to be divided with paths into squares and triangles, and embellished with a fountain, urns and pergolas trailing with roses. At the moment though this area of the garden awaits a sensitive decision over its future – it is one of

Below left: The tone at Thornton Manor's 20th-century gardens is largely classical with loggias, pavilions & pillars. Below right: A doorway through a decorative loggia leads from the beautiful terraces to the kitchen garden.

the places under consideration for the spa's car park, but a rather more appealing idea for conservationists is that it could be used to produce high quality food for the guests.

By the time the title of Lord Leverhulme died with Philip, the 3rd Viscount, the benevolently patriarchal principles that had made his grandfather one of the most famous employers in the country already seemed alien to a working world dominated by freelancers, consultants, the self-employed, or career changes every couple of years. Yet in spite of these disparate attitudes, few cannot be struck by the legacy of the first Viscount Leverhulme, whose creation at Port Sunlight is both beautiful and inspiring, and whose gardens at Thornton Manor are such a wonderfully-preserved example of the Arts and Crafts style.

Select Bibliography

English Heritage Register of Parks and Gardens of Special Historic Interest, 1999.

George, WL. *Engines of Social Progress.* Adam and Charles Black, London, 1907.

Lever, William Hesketh. *Co-Partnership: An Address.* Port Sunlight, 1912.

Mawson, Thomas H. *Civic Art: Studies in Town Planning, Parks, Boulevards and Open Spaces.* BT Batsford, London, 1940.

Mawson, Thomas H and Mawson, E Prentice. *The Art and Craft of Garden Making.* 1900, BT Batsford, London, 5th edition, 1926.

Mawson, Thomas H. *The Life and Work of an English Landscape Architect: An Autobiography.* The Richards Press, London, 1927.

Meacham, Standish. *Regaining Paradise: Englishness and the Early Garden City Movement.* Yale University Press, USA, 1999.

References

1   Standish Meacham. *Regaining Paradise: Englishness and the Early Garden City Movement.* 1999, p31.
2   William Hesketh Lever. *Co-Partnership: An Address.* 1912, p24.
3   WL George, *Engines of Social Progress,* 1907, p115.
4   Thomas H Mawson. *Civic Art: Studies in Town Planning, Parks, Boulevards and Open Spaces.* 1940, p280.
5   Thomas H Mawson, *Civic Art: Studies in Town Planning, Parks, Boulevards and Open Spaces.* 1940, p284.
6   William Hesketh Lever. *Co-Partnership: An Address.* 1912, p3.
7   *English Heritage Register of Parks and Gardens of Special Historic Interest,* 1999.
8   *English Heritage Register of Parks and Gardens of Special Historic Interest,* 1999.
9   Thomas H Mawson. *The Life and Work of an English Landscape Architect: An Autobiography.* 1927, p116.
10   Thomas H Mawson. *The Life and Work of an English Landscape Architect: An Autobiography.* 1927, p117.
11   Thomas H Mawson. *The Life and Work of an English Landscape Architect: An Autobiography.* 1927, p190.
12   Standish Meacham. *Regaining Paradise: Englishness and the Early Garden City Movement.* 1999, p17.
13   Thomas H Mawson. *The Life and Work of an English Landscape Architect: An Autobiography.* 1927, p180.
14   Thomas H Mawson and E Prentice Mawson, 1900, *The Art and Craft of Garden Making.* 5th edition, 1926, p204.
15   Thomas H Mawson. *The Life and Work of an English Landscape Architect: An Autobiography,* 1927, illus. 25 and 26.
16   *English Heritage Register of Parks and Gardens of Special Historic Interest,* 1999.
17   Thomas H Mawson and E Prentice Mawson. 1900, *The Art and Craft of Garden Making.* 5th edition, 1926, p261.
18   Thomas H Mawson and E Prentice Mawson. 1900, *The Art and Craft of Garden Making.* 5th edition, 1926, p264.
19   Thomas H Mawson and E Prentice Mawson. *1900, The Art and Craft of Garden Making.* 5th edition, 1926, p255.

Tirley Garth, Tarporley

*T*he Arts and Crafts style is still one of Britain's favourites, with its nostalgic attention to detail and romantic visions making it a very intimate approach to architecture and garden design. A fantastic example of this is Tirley Garth, Tarporley which, having been beautifully preserved during the last century, is a real treasure. Tirley's situation on a hilly ridge combines gentle countryside with stunning views south across the Cheshire Plain of the dramatic hill castles of Beeston and Peckforton. Its rural quiet is nevertheless under ten miles from Chester and so it was the ideal location to build a new home for Bryan Leesmith, a director of the local chemical firm Brunner Mond (soon to become ICI, still a dominant force in this part of Cheshire). Having chosen the spot, Leesmith commissioned the Arts and Crafts architect CE Mallows to design the house and garden, and as Mallows shared London offices with leading landscape architect Thomas Mawson, it was inevitable that Mawson's touch should be felt at Tirley also.

Mallows was a passionate believer that in order to create unity of design, gardens should be designed by an architect as a whole with the house. In an influential article in *The Studio*, a fashionable design magazine, he demonstrated his appreciation of the garden styles of history, showing in particular an admiration of the architectural and European-influenced approach of the Renaissance: 'In the house and garden architecture of this period there is a unity and completeness of effect which approaches very near perfection; and this, it should be observed, is altogether irrespective of the charm of associations and interest of time; it is a matter of design entirely – the happy union of house and garden in architectural design. The secret of the success of this work is very easily discovered; it lies in the fact that the designers of those days considered the whole problem

Top: The house at Tirley Garth blends perfectly with its garden.
Inset: A boy with flute plays near the house.

*A valley, planted largely with rhododendrons,
mends its way below the house.*

Lavatera evokes Tirley Garth's quintessentially English feel.

Tirley Garth is rarely open to visitors & so retains a sense of quiet seclusion.

of home design and the distribution of the various parts of the ground surrounding it as one complete work, where each detail took its right place as an indispensable part of the whole.'[1] Mallows' approach to garden design placed it firmly, if sometimes controversially, within the province of the building designer.

Mallows began work at Tarporley in 1907, designing a beautiful house around a calming internal courtyard – the 'Garth' from which Tirley gets its name. This square area is bordered on all sides by stone cloisters and has in the centre a sunken fountain pool lined with blue tiling, which is adorned with bright flowers in summer. Writing in *The Studio* in 1909, Mallows described the role of this courtyard: 'The point of central interest, it will be seen, is the cloister court, which has been planned with as much care as possible in relation to both house and garden, so that interesting views of each can be obtained at given points. At the entrance from the carriage court, for example, a small picture of the cloister garth, with its bright flowers and fountain pool in the centre, is obtained through the shade of the arched entrance way which is vaulted with a flat curved barrel vault.'[2] True to Mallows' intention, this introduction to Tirley does indeed capture the visitor's attention and sets the tone for the entire visit as the main entrance to the house is via the Garth's cloisters. Sadly though, the views from the Garth are one of the very few aspects of Tirley to have suffered since its conception: that to the north, which would once have led to the orchard, is now crudely blocked by an ugly timber shed erected hard against the external wall of the courtyard.

There can be no doubt that an immense amount of money was pumped into the construction of this enchanting house: the woodwork is carved with huge attention to detail, tiles unique to Tirley Garth are used throughout, and each room is crammed with enough architectural details to occupy the attention for hours on end. Yet this family home is at no point intimidating. Rather than being intended as a statement of its owner's wealth and power, as we see in so many earlier buildings, it is small

in scale and reassuringly welcoming in spirit, favouring intimate rooms and twisting corridors over high ceilings and grand entrances.

However, Mr Leesmith had to sell the property before it was completed and so ownership passed in 1912 to Brunner Mond who leased it to Richard Henry Prestwich, a businessman who relocated his family from Manchester to his new rural residence. In spite of the turmoil in its ownership, construction went on and a stunning garden developed in which Mr Prestwich's contribution was instrumental. Tirley Garth was not destined to be a family home however, as Mr Prestwich's daughter Irene joined the Campaign for Moral Re-Armament group, a Christian organisation based on the principles of honesty, purity, unselfishness and love, that has its roots in The Oxford Group. In 1940 she invited the organisation to shelter from the war at Tirley Garth, an experience which she described in her memoir: 'I saw my home with throngs of people coming with their problems and going out with God. And I walked home on air with a new hope. This was what I was meant to do with my life, and my home, to bring change to thousands.'[3] After the war, Miss Prestwich presented Tirley Garth to the MRA, having used almost all her inherited wealth to buy the property from ICI, from whom the Prestwich family had always been renting it. Dedicated to the MRA and to the Tirley Garth Trust that arose from her donation, this determined woman continued to live at Tirley Garth until her death in 1974. Partly by accident, partly by design, the Trust made few changes to the property over the last century, and so it has remained a living museum to the Arts and Crafts tradition.

The terraced formal gardens sit to the south and east of the house, beginning alongside the cobbled turning circle, with a sunken garden based around a charming fountain depicting a boy and flute with frog. From here the visitor passes to a crazy-paved terrace in which are four rectangular grass parterres bordered with roses. In fact, Mallows' original plans for this terrace show a slightly different design, laid out with two small beds sandwiched between two larger ones. An aerial photograph of Tirley Garth, thought to be from the 1920s, shows the lay-out as it is today, so it is probable that the original designs were modified almost immediately.[4] Also surviving are cropping plans from when Tirley Garth was planted with produce by the Land Army in the Second World War. Every inch of the gardens seems to have been put to good use, and the 1941 plan shows this terrace to have been planted with beet.[5] The memoir of Irene Prestwich gives a glimpse of life at Tirley Garth at this time, describing the effect of one of many air raids on Liverpool and Manchester: 'We were blacked out, and never hit, but that night [28th November 1940] thirty-six incendiary bombs fell in our garden – one on the terrace within six feet of the house, and one on the roof ... Next day was the 21st birthday of one of the girls who worked in the vegetable garden; and round her cake, the bases of twenty-one incendiary bombs made excellent candlesticks.'[6]

From the terrace some generous circular steps, typical of this period, lead down to a lawn which sweeps towards the view over the Cheshire Plain before dropping steeply to what inspection reveals to be a rhododendron valley. At the foot of the retaining terrace wall are two herbaceous borders. Detailed planting plans by either Mallows or Mawson show these yew-framed borders to have been filled with walled plants such as *Ceanothus G. de Versailles*, *Choisya ternata*, *Vitis coignetiae*, and *Clematis Jackmanii*, and border plants such as hollyhocks, delphiniums, irises and paeonies.[7] In recent years a student working at Tirley decided to use these plans to restore the borders, which, as borders do, had gradually evolved over the years till there was little resemblance to the original planting. To her dismay however, she discovered that over the century, British horti-

*Tirley Garth's layout has changed little from this 1920s
aerial photograph (Tirley Garth Trust).*

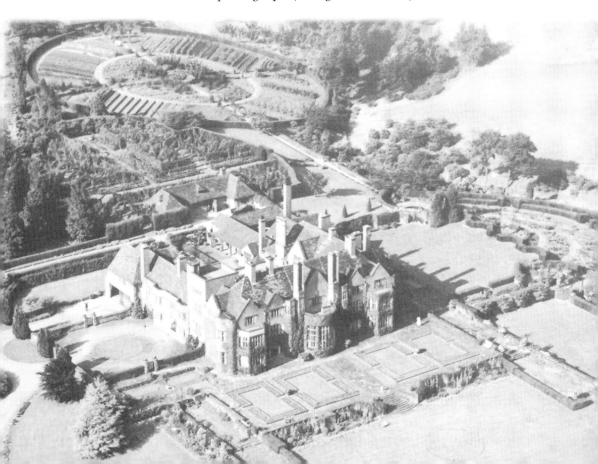

culture has developed so dramatically that only a couple of the original plants still exist, the others now replaced with varieties more appealing to the modern gardener.

Following the house walls round the corner to the east, the gardens, consisting of a series of rooms based on geometric shapes and linked by narrow walks (such as that bordered by hydrangeas), are set out on terraces at a slightly lower level from the house. Here are two enclosed square lawns, each bordered by a rural wall where large rough slabs rest to form the effect of the balustrade having been placed there almost by accident. Each is entered via a rustic wooden gate and is attractive enough to be a garden in itself, but they were in fact designed as a pair of tennis courts. A curved staircase from this corner leads the visitor round a covered pool down to the rhododendron valley.

To the north of here is the octagonal garden where a charming fountain is set in an enclosed hedged area. Over the years this area had drifted away from its original concept but recently the team at Tirley have reinstated Mallows' spirit by repositioning wooden pillars planted with climbing roses to create an octagonal pergola. Here too is a recent alpine garden, created as a gesture of thanks to a generous donor to the Tirley Garth Trust.

Beyond this area is a remarkable rose garden in which seven semi-circular terraces of grass and rose beds steadily descend the slope from the house towards the rhododendron valley, framed by well-clipped yew rings.

Gardeners rue the fact that the summer beauty of roses comes with the cost of their spiky ugliness in winter, but the careful architectural shaping of these beds makes them striking even in the absence of flowers and foliage.

A Spring Walk leads north from the rose garden and is bisected by a romantic flight of steps leading down to the stream from what was once the orchard but is now the car park. These wide stone steps are bowed in a way that belies their relatively youthful age and so somehow demand a detour up them from the Spring Walk. Sadly though, it is today a disappointment to reach the top of this flight to find only a gravel car park where there should be welcoming fruit trees.

The Spring Walk next leads to another framed area that was originally intended as the kitchen garden and is known as the Round Acre because of its distinctive circular shape. Two axial paths dissect the hedged circle into quarters and as the current planting of grass and flowering cherries is sparse, the immense scale of the geometric area can be appreciated in a way that makes it strangely moving. At the north exit to the Round Acre is a gardener's fairytale wooden Bothy, one of many charming buildings within the grounds. It is arguably this part of the Tirley Garth gardens that leaves the greatest impression on the visitor today. This would have pleased Mallows who had been keen that the productive areas of gardens were not neglected, writing of the kitchen garden that it has a 'large semi-circular end,

Above: The rose garden is built of seven semi-circular terraces descending the slope from the house.

[in fact, it was eventually constructed as a full circle] around which a wide walk has been planned, connected on its western side with the centre of the cloister court in the house plan, and on its eastern side with the pergola … A hint of this semicircular termination to the kitchen garden is given in the distance. In this way the kitchen-garden, which ought always to be one of the most beautiful parts in any garden scheme, is connected with the rest of the design and made a partition of the pleasure-gardens, instead of being relegated as a disconnected and unsightly fragment to some obscure portion of the grounds.'[8]

Running alongside the bottom of the perched garden terraces is a hidden valley through which a stream flows past dense plantings of rhododendrons and azaleas. The Mallows garden plan drawn up for Mr Prestwich shows this stream to have seven pools and one pond but, if created, these are now largely lost as the stream is nearly silted up.[9] There are now huge numbers of rhododendrons at Tirley Garth, with designs by TH Mawson specifying planting in front of the rose garden of a huge *Rhododendron* 'Pink Pearl', as well as *Rhododendron* 'Doncaster', the rosy purple of *Rhododendron* 'Lord Derby', and the white *Rhododendron* 'Mrs J. Clutton'. This particular area was to be planted around the edge with azaleas, alpines, and ericas. The reliance of the gardens on rhododendrons has caused problems for the garden staff – they have to be heavily clipped every few years, resulting in a very forlorn scene that season. In recent years however, Head Gardener Tony Booth developed a routine of clipping the bushes from underneath so that the ugly pruned branches were shielded by the older foliage, which in turn could later be trimmed once the foliage underneath had grown back. In spite of the trouble they may cause, the rhododendrons are in many ways the toast of Tirley Garth, their qualities as garden shrubs being exhalted by Thomas Mawson in *The Art and Craft of Garden Making*: 'The hybrids of some of the hardy species are generally admitted to be the finest of all our hardy shrubs, being exceedingly ornamental and showing to great advantage when planted in groups and masses; embrac-

The garden's design is based on geometric shapes,
such as around this octagonal pergola.

ing, as they do, every shade of colour from the purest white to the richest crimson and purple, the rich colours of some varieties being simply magnificent. When not in bloom, rhododendrons are really fine shrubs, having the advantage of being evergreen and possessing splendid foliage.'[10] The atmospheric paths of this valley can be followed almost to the end of the site, where the main drive from the house ends in sturdy stone pillars to the Utkinton-Willington road. This drive had been the subject of some discussion between Mallows and Mawson, now standing, as Mawson wished, slightly away from that in Mallows' original design.[11]

I visited Tirley Garth in the autumn of 2002, only weeks before it was sold to Mersey Television because it had become surplus to the requirements of the MRA (now changing its name to Initiatives of Change). It was then, as it had always been, in impeccable condition. It is not for me to question what Irene Prestwich would have felt about the sale of the home that she gave so generously to the Campaign for Moral Re-Armament, but we can at least expect that this remarkable Arts and Crafts treasure, surviving almost in its original form, will continue to be preserved in its pristine condition, as it was apparently this which endeared it to its buyers. In her memoir, Miss Prestwich wrote of the emotional difficulties she overcame in passing on her family home to the care of others when she gave it to the MRA. I hope that she will not be disappointed now: 'It was not altogether an easy transition for me, in spite of my warm welcome for it. I had to learn, not without some doubt and difficulty, to trust people … to carry out the practical work of the house as part of their duty.'[12]

Select Bibliography

Aslet, Clive. 'Tirley Garth, Cheshire'. *Country Life*, 18th March 1982, p702-5.
English Heritage Register of Parks and Gardens of Special Historic Interest, 2002.
Mallows, CE. 'Architectural Gardening, with illustrations after designs by CE Mallows FRIBA'. *The Studio*, Number 44, June-September 1908, p187.
Mallows, CE. 'Architectural Gardening - II, with illustrations after designs by CE Mallows FRIBA'. *The Studio*, Number 45, October 1908-January 1909, p31-42.
Mawson, Thomas H. *The Art and Craft of Garden Making*. T. Batsford, London, 1900.
Mawson, Thomas H. *The Life and Work of an English Landscape Architect: An Autobiography*, The Richards Press, London, 1927.
Prestwich, Irene. *Irene Prestwich of Tirley Garth: A Personal Memoir*. Grosvenor Books, London, 1971.
Tirley Garth, Near Tarporley, Cheshire, (Sale Catalogue). Jackson-Stops and Staff, Chester, 2002.
Wigan, Virginia. *about Tirley Garth….* The Tirley Garth Trust, Cheshire, 1999.

The archive material used here was held at Tirley Garth until the property's sale in 2002.

References

1 CE Mallows, 'Architectural Gardening, with illustrations after designs by CE Mallows FRIBA', *The Studio*, Number 44, June-September 1908, p187.
2 CE Mallows, 'Architectural Gardening - II, with illustrations after designs by CE Mallows FRIBA', *The Studio*, Number 45, October 1908-January 1909, p36.
3 Irene Prestwich, *Irene Prestwich of Tirley Garth: A Personal Memoir*, 1971, p10.
4 This photograph was held at Tirley Garth until its sale in 2002.
5 'Cropping Chart, 1941'.
6 Irene Prestwich, *Irene Prestwich of Tirley Garth: A Personal Memoir*, 1971, p16.
7 'Terrace Borders, Tirley Garth'.
8 CE Mallows, 'Architectural Gardening, with illustrations after designs by CE Mallows FRIBA', *The Studio*, Number 44, June-September 1908, p187.
9 CE Mallows, 'Plan: Tirley Garth, Cheshire for RH Prestwick Esq'.
10 Thomas H Mawson, *The Art and Craft of Garden Making*, 1900, p146.
11 TH Mawson, 'Plan Showing Proposed Planting Along Drive of Tirley Garth for RH Prestwick Esq' and 'Proposed Planting of Drive of Tirlie Garth', initialled THM.
12 Irene Prestwich, *Irene Prestwich of Tirley Garth: A Personal Memoir*, 1971, p13.

Index

A

Adam, W 53,
Adlington Hall 6, 7, *42-49*
Archer, Kelvin 112
Arley Hall 34, 68, *82-90*
Armstrong, Les 72, 74, 75, 76
Ashbrook, 10th Viscount (Desmond Flowers) 84
Ashbrook, 11th Viscount (Michael Flowers) 82, 89
Ashbrook, Elizabeth Viscountess (Elizabeth Egerton-Warburton) 84, 88
Ashbrook, Viscountess (Zoë), 82, 88, 89

B

Badeslade, Thomas 73, 78
Bakewell, Robert 20, 23, *24*
Balfour, Professor Isaac Bayley 152, 153, 154
Bardwell, Thomas 42
Barry, Edward 96
Bateman, James 85, 86
Bees Limited 152, 153, 154, 155
Biddulph Grange 85
Birkenhead Park 7, 64, *114-121*, 122
Blow, Detmar 74, 75
Booth, Lady Mary 36
Booth, 'Old' Sir George 32
Booth, Tony 171
Booth, 'Young' Sir George 32
Brayford, Bill 23, 25
Brereton Hall, 68
Brooks, Harry 142
Brooks, Juliet 144
Brooks, Randle 142, 144, 146
Brunner Mond 166, 168
Bulley, Arthur Kilpin 150, *152*, 153, 154, 155
Burke, Sir Bernard 50
Burton Manor 160

C

Caldwells Nursery 68
Campaign for Moral Re-Armament 168, 172
Capesthorne Manor 68
Carr and Caldwell Nursery 37
Catchpole, Steve 46, 47, 48

Cheshire Life 125
Cholmondeley Castle *18-29*
Cholmondeley, 1st Earl of (Hugh Cholmondeley) 18, 20
Cholmondeley, 3rd Earl of (George Cholmondeley) 22
Cholmondeley, 1st Marquess of (George James Cholmondeley) 20, 21, 22, 23
Cholmondeley, 6th Marquess of (Hugh Cholmondeley) 25
Cholmondeley, Lavinia Marchioness of 23, 25
Cook, Paul 154, 155, 156
Cooper, Roland Edgar 154, 155
Country Life 55, 70, 73, 74, 84, 86, 89, 93, 94, *95*, 101
Crewe, 1st Baron Crewe of 92, 93
Crewe, 3rd Baron (Hungerford Crewe) 92, 93, 94, 96
Crewe Hall 7, *91-97*
Crewe, Sir Randulph 91
Cunnington, Peter 154

D

Dennys, John 70
Dorfold Hall 8, *98-105*
Douglas and Fordham 159
Douglas, John 74, 124
Downes, William 20
Dunham Massey 7, *30-41*, 52, 68

E

Eaton Hall 8, *70-81*, 124
Egerton, 2nd Baron (Wilbraham Egerton) 64
Egerton, 3rd Baron (Alan de Tatton Egerton) 65, 66
Egerton, 4th Baron (Maurice de Tatton Egerton) 58, 66, 64
Egerton, John 58
Egerton, Lady Anna 58, 66
Egerton, Philip 21
Egerton, Samuel 60
Egerton, Sir Thomas 58
Egerton, Wilbraham 64
Egerton-Warburton, Antoinette 84
Egerton-Warburton, Elizabeth - see

Ashbrook, Elizabeth Viscountess
Egerton-Warburton, Rowland and Mary 84,
    85, 86, 88
Elgood, George S 84, 85
Ellis, David Williams *110, 106*
Emes, William 7, 21, 22, 60, 82, 84, 92, 144
Everson, Paul 12, 13

F

Farrer, Reginald 155
Fitton, Edward III 12
Fitton, Edward V 12
Fitton, Mary 12
Forrest, George 153, 154, 155
Foster, Charles and Jane 89
Fukuhara, Professor Masao 66
Fuller, Thomas 91

G

Garbutt, Mike 120
Gardener's Chronicle 23, 73, 74, 76, 92, 94
Gawsworth New Hall 10
Gawsworth Old Hall 7, *10-17*
George, WL 158
Gerard, Charles (Earl of Macclesfield) 12
Gibbs, Vicary 56
Gladstone, Henry 160
Groby, Lord Grey of (George Harry Grey)
    37 38
Grosvenor Park 7, *122-125*, 128
Grosvenor, Sir Thomas 70

H

Hall, Joseph Compton 33
Hall, SC 100
Hamilton, 4th Duke of (James Douglas) 12
Harrington, 1st Earl of (William Stanhope) 12
Harrington, 11th Earl of (William Stanhope)
    12
Harris, John *31*, 33, 34, 41
Hollier, Glen 128, 133
Hope, John 108
Hope, Josiah 153
Hornblower, Lewis 118
Hough Hole House - see Mellor's Gardens
Houghton, Lord 96
Hulme, Ken 155

Humphries, Gordon and Ruth 137
Humphries, Philip 96

J

Jekyll, Gertrude 75, 84, 85, 86

K

Kemp, Edward 7, 54, 116, 122,128, 129,130
Kendall, Graham 37
Kenworthy, Jonathan 73
Kip, Johannes 30, 32, 33
Knyff, Leonard 30, 32, 33

L

Lady Lever Art Gallery *158*, 159
Lathan, George 84
Latimer, George 129
Leah, Allan 129
Leesmith, Bryan 166, 168
Legh, Camilla 47, 48
Legh, Charles 42, 46, 47, 48
Legh, Peter IX 53
Legh, Peter XII 53
Legh, Piers I 52
Legh, Richard 52
Legh, Thomas 53
Lennox-Boyd, Arabella *70, 71*, 72, 73, 75
Leoni, Giacomo 53
Lever, William Hesketh - see Leverhulme, 1st
    Viscount
Leverhulme, 1st Viscount (William Hesketh
    Lever) 7, 157, 158, 159, 160, 161, 162,
    165
Leverhulme, 3rd Viscount (Philip Leverhulme)
    160, 161, 164, 165
Lightfoot, Nick 164
London and North Western Railway Com-
    pany (LNWR) 126, 130
London, George 18
Loudon, John Claudius 67
Lutyens, Edwin 75
Lyme Park 6, *50-57*

M

Macclesfield Courier and Herald 136, 137
Macclesfield, Earl of - see Gerard, Charles
Magner, Lee and Janet 160

Mainwaring, Ellen 144
Mainwaring, Emily 144
Mainwaring, Henry 144
Mainwaring, Sir Philip Tatton 144
Mainwaring, Thomas 144
Mallows, CE 166, 168, 169, 170, 171, 172
Marbury Hall *84*, 88
Martin, EH 93, 100
Massey, Hamo de 30
Mawson, Thomas 7, 158, 159, 160, 161, 164, 166, 169, 171, 172
Mellor, James 134, 136, 137, 139, 140
Mellor's Gardens (Hough Hole House) *134-141*
Milner, Edward 64
Mohun, Charlotte Lady 12
Mohun, 5th Lord (Charles Mohun) 12
Moon, Sir Richard 130
Mow Cop 6, *108*

N

Nates, Claude 53
Nesfield, William Andrews 7, 73, 88, 93, 94, 95, 97, 98, 100, 101, *110*, 112
Ness Botanic Gardens 6, 7, *150-156*
Newton, 1st Baron (William John Legh) 54
Newton, 2nd Baron (Thomas Wodehouse Legh) 56
Newton, 3rd Baron (Richard William Davenport Legh) 56
Newton, Lady Evelyn 56
Newton, Lady Helen 56
Norris, John 33
North, William 36

O

Offley, John 92
Oldbury, Mary - see Warrington, Countess Mary
Oldham, Dave 144
Olmsted, Frederick Law 76, 118, 119, 120
Ormerod, George 13, 49, 69, *91*, 93
Oulton Park 21, 84

P

Paxton, Joseph 7, 58, 64, 65, 118, 116
Peover Hall 6, 68, *142-149*

Port Sunlight *157-159*
Prestwich, Irene 168, 169, 172
Prestwich, Richard Henry 168, 171
Probert, HW 133
Public Walks, Select Committee on 114, 116

Q

Queen's Park 7, *126-133*

R

Raynsford, Gary 53, 54, 56
Repton, Humphry 7, 58, 60, *61*, 92, 97, 108
Richards, Elizabeth 12
Richards, Monica 12
Richards, Raymond 12
Richards, Timothy 12, 14, 15
Robertson, John 118
Rode Hall 7, *106-113*
Russell, Misses 137

S

Salvin, Anthony *83*, 84
Seymour, Lady Charlotte 23
Shipbroke, Baron of (Richard de Vernon) 91
Simpson, James Lomax 159, 164
Smith, Raymond 73, 75
Smith, Vernon Russell 75
St Lawrence's Church, Peover *144, 145*
Stamford, 4th Earl of (Harry Grey) 36
Stamford, 5th Earl of (George Harry Grey) 34, 36, 37
Stamford, 6th Earl of (George Harry Grey) 37
Stamford, 7th Earl of (George Harry Grey) 37, 38
Stamford, 8th Earl of (Rev. Harry Grey) 38
Stamford, 9th Earl of (William Grey) 33, 38
Stamford, 10th Earl of (Roger Grey) 38
Stamford Park, Altrincham 118
Stokes, George 65
Stuart Thomas, Graham 56
Studio, The 166, 168

T

Tabley Hall 68, 108
Tatton Park, 6, 7, *58-69*
Thelwall Hall 106
Thornton Hough 159

Thornton Manor 6, *157, 159-165*
Tijou, Jean 20, 25
Tirley Garth 7, *166-172*
Tirley Garth Trust 168, 170
Tollemache, Wilbraham and Ann Spencer 98, 100
Tomkinson, James 98
Tomkinson, Rev. James 98
Turner, JMW 108
Turner, Richard 12, 13, 14, 137
Turner, William 22

V

van Diest, Adrien 30, 32, 33
van Nost, John 20

W

Walpole, Horace 20
Warburton, Sir Peter (4th Baronet) 82
Warburton, Sir Peter (5th Baronet) 82
Ward, Frank Kingdon 154, 155
Warrington, 1st Earl of (Henry Booth) 32
Warrington, 2nd Earl of (George Booth) 32, 33, 34, 36
Warrington, Countess Mary (Mary Oldbury) 32
Waterhouse, Alfred 74
Watts, W 53
Webb, Francis William 126, 130

Webb, John 7, 22, 62, 72, 108, 109
Wellcome Corporation 91, 92, 96
Westminster, 1st Duke of (Hugh Lupus Grosvenor) 70, 74, 77, 75
Westminster, 6th Duke of (Gerald Cavendish Grosvenor) 70, 75, 76
Westminster, Duchess of (Natalia) 70, 72, 75, 76
Westminster, 1st Marquess of (Robert Grosvenor) 70
Westminster, 2nd Marquess of (Richard Grosvenor) 70, *122*
Whitaker, Mr. 92, 93
Wilbraham, Lady Baker (Ann) 110, 112
Wilbraham, Mary Bootle 108
Wilbraham, Ralph 100
Wilbraham, Randle I 106
Wilbraham, Randle II 106, 108
Wilbraham, Randle III 108
Wilbraham, Randle IV 110
Wilbraham, Richard Bootle 108
Wilbraham, Roger 106
Wilbraham, Sir Richard Baker 106, 108, 109, 112
Wyatt, Lewis 53, 54, 56, *57*, 58, 62, 108
Wyatt, Samuel 58

Y

Youd, Sam 66

Places are marked in bold
Illustrations are marked in italics